CLOSER TO GOD

Books by
Jeannie Cunnion

Closer to God

Don't Miss Out

Mom Set Free

Parenting the Wholehearted Child

CLOSER TO GOD

A 40-DAY PURSUIT OF GOD'S PERSONAL PRESENCE

JEANNIE CUNNION

BETHANYHOUSE
a division of Baker Publishing Group
Minneapolis, Minnesota

Published by Bethany House Publishers
Minneapolis, Minnesota
BethanyHouse.com

Bethany House Publishers is a division of
Baker Publishing Group, Grand Rapids, Michigan

Printed in the United States of America

Library of Congress Cataloging-in-Publication Data
Names: Cunnion, Jeannie, author.
Title: Closer to God : a 40-day pursuit of God's personal presence / Jeannie Cunnion.
Description: Minneapolis, Minnesota : Bethany House Publishers, a division of Baker Publishing Group, [2024] | Includes bibliographical references.
Identifiers: LCCN 2023057175 | ISBN 9780764238475 (cloth) | ISBN 9781493447992 (epub)
Subjects: LCSH: Meditations. | Christian life.
Classification: LCC BV4832.3 .C86 2024 | DDC 242/.2—dc23/eng/20240224
LC record available at https://lccn.loc.gov/2023057175

Cover design by Christopher Gilbert, Studio Gearbox
Cover image from Shutterstock
Author photo © Meshali Mitchell

The author is represented by the literary agency of Wolgemuth & Associates.

Baker Publishing Group publications use paper produced from sustainable forestry practices and postconsumer waste whenever possible.

24 25 26 27 28 29 30 7 6 5 4 3 2 1

CONTENTS

KEY PASSAGE

Indeed, I count everything as loss because of the surpassing worth of knowing Christ Jesus my Lord. For his sake I have suffered the loss of all things and count them as rubbish, in order that I may gain Christ and be found in him, not having a righteousness of my own that comes from the law, but that which comes through faith in Christ, the righteousness from God that depends on faith—that I may know him and the power of his resurrection, and may share his sufferings, becoming like him in his death, that by any means possible I may attain the resurrection from the dead.

Philippians 3:8–11

INTRODUCTION

"I *still* want more, God."

This devotional was born from that prayer.

And this is the story behind it:

Several years ago I experienced a fresh longing for God. This longing wasn't birthed out of a special situation or a particular hardship as much as it was just an increasing awareness of how much I need Him and a growing gratitude for His incomparable love. The longer I follow Jesus, the more aware I become of what an absolute miracle it is that He loves me and gave His life to rescue me. My longing led me to pray simple but sincere prayers like "I want all of you, God! I want to know you better. I want to rely on you more. I want all you will give of yourself to me! Whatever it takes, have your way in me."

God answered my prayers, which I now understand He himself birthed in me, by creating a deep curiosity about the Holy Spirit within me. While I understood the Holy Spirit had been dwelling in me since the day I put my trust in Jesus almost forty years earlier, I had very little understanding of the magnitude of His role in my life. So essentially, God was preparing to re-introduce me to the One I'd been neglecting so I could enjoy the benefits of His presence that I'd been forfeiting. He was inviting me not only to know but also to experience His personal presence *in* me in a radically new way.

Over the last several years, as I've experienced more of His personal presence by welcoming the work of the Holy Spirit in my life, I've increasingly desired to go deeper still. Not to get things *from* God but to get more *of* God. The *more* I've longed for is God himself. His presence!

And what's beautifully clear in Scripture, which God highlighted for me in my longing for Him, is that the path to God's personal presence is paved with the practicing of repentance and the pursuit of holiness.

Yes, *repentance* and *holiness*, two good things that often get a bad rap but that are actually utterly life-giving and freedom-bringing!

I should mention that I was raised as a preacher's kid in a home that very much taught me these truths. I've had what you might call a healthy relationship with repentance and a solid understanding of the Christian's call to holiness. But what I didn't appreciate, until the Spirit illuminated it, is that the deeper intimacy I craved with God would be an invitation to exalt King Jesus in areas of my life that I hadn't truly surrendered. It was as if God was asking me, "How *much* do you want more intimacy with me? What self-centered living still needs to be surrendered to me?" This isn't about striving to live perfectly. Far from it, my friend. This is about allowing the perfection of Jesus that covers us to wreck us and purify our desires and draw us into His presence and conform us into His likeness! God's love for us isn't based on our loyalty to Him. Jesus took care of that. Please hear me say I still miss the mark every day in a myriad of ways. I will never outgrow my need for grace. I only become more aware of how desperately I need it. And this awareness is what creates in me a desire to go deeper still.

See, though you and I may not personally know each other, we can be sure of this one thing *about* each other: We were created with a desire for a *deep* life. Our souls long to know and be known by God, to be in intimate, deeply personal, vibrant relationship with the Divine. We were made to both stand in awe of His holiness *and* relax our shoulders in the safety of His love. You are not the exception to this truth. I am not the exception to this truth. There is no asterisk to this sentence, pointing us to fine print at the end of this book explaining why certain people don't qualify for or desire a deeper life with God. Everything we chase or fix our attention on is an attempt to satisfy a longing, a deep-seated ache, a groaning to know God's wondrous withness.

But sadly, the message that in Him alone (alone!) will our unsatisfied souls find satisfaction can become so familiar that it gets lost on us. Or we become numb to it because we've chosen to keep chasing lesser things.

"I know, I know" might be our instinctual response to being told we were designed to enjoy a deep life with God—meanwhile many of us are sleepwalking our way through our relationship with Him. But I believe the Spirit of God desires to awaken us to a relationship with God that is marked by awe and anticipation of His activity in our lives. The Spirit of God desires to, and is fully able to, help us experience God intimately, to know how beautiful and beyond comprehension the assurance of His presence truly is.

I've written this devotional to help us cultivate intimacy with God. To know, *really* know, His withness. We will discover what God says will draw us deeper into His presence, and how we can invite the lover of our souls to have His rightful place in our lives. But for us to enjoy His glorious presence, we will need the Holy Spirit to create in us the same holy hunger, humility, and posture of heart Paul had when he penned our key passage, Philippians 3:8–11, printed at the beginning of this devotional for easy reference.

Let's read it together.

> Indeed, I count everything as loss because of the surpassing worth of knowing Christ Jesus my Lord. For his sake I have suffered the loss of all things and count them as rubbish, in order that I may gain Christ and be found in him, not having a righteousness of my own that comes from the law, but that which comes through faith in Christ, the righteousness from God that depends on faith—that I may know him and the power of his resurrection, and may share his sufferings, becoming like him in his death, that by any means possible I may attain the resurrection from the dead.
>
> Philippians 3:8–11

This is the passage on which we will build, and the one to which we will often return. We will pray that Jesus, by His Spirit, will allow us to "know Him and the power of His resurrection" (v. 10) in a fresh and profound way. That we would, like Paul, see how the worth of knowing Christ, being found in Him, and being covered in His righteousness, surpasses all else we seek. And that a deeper life in His presence will be ours through the Holy Spirit.

Our openness to the Holy Spirit will be essential throughout these forty days together because a primary role of the Holy Spirit is to make Jesus increasingly beautiful and irresistible to us. The Holy Spirit increases and intensifies our awareness of God's withness, and leaves us awestricken at the life-altering intimacy of the Trinity we are invited into when we put our trust in Jesus. This is what the Spirit is doing in me as I grow (albeit often slowly and sometimes stubbornly) in my willingness to yield to His leadership in my life.

I am so grateful for and humbled by this, and I want to assure you of something you will find reiterated throughout this devotional: I surrender all to Jesus because He laid down His life to save me and to make me a new creation in Him, crowning me with the identity of a child of the King!

So I am going to use whatever breath He continues to put in my lungs to help us encounter our living God who loves us with a breathtaking love. To shine the light on the wondrous and glorious gift of himself. He is worthy of our full adoration because He gave us His Son to bring us back into intimate relationship with Him. Relationship that, by the way, we ruined. He could have chosen rejection but instead He chose rescue.

What unfathomable love He has for us! He didn't give us His Son to keep us at arm's length. He gave us Jesus to bring us back into the intimacy of His presence.

Now before we dig in, can we name the elephant in the room? Putting the word *intimacy* and Jesus in the same sentence makes some of us squirm (awkward!) because of the physical, even sexual, connotation that intimacy carries. So I am going to give us the definition of intimacy, with a lot of other descriptive words, to help us usher the elephant out of the room and back to the zoo. Or I guess I should say the savanna.

Intimacy is the state of being in a very personal relationship. It's *that* normal.

Words similar to intimacy include:

- *close familiarity*
- *friendship*
- *fellowship*
- *companionship*
- *togetherness*
- *belonging*
- *love*
- *nearness*
- *mutual affection*
- *closeness*

These are the words that I pray will characterize our relationship with God at the close of our forty days because this is the life we were made for! I'm excited to go deeper still with you into the beauty and mystery of intimacy with God!

What Can You Expect?

Come ready for a feast—a substantive meal to linger over. Growing closer to God requires time spent with God. Vibrancy and depth come from time in His presence, not from checking the boxes. I can say that with confidence because I've tried the latter approach. It doesn't work.

Over the next forty days we will engage with daily devotions that will invite us to

- practice repentance that leads to the refreshment of our souls;
- pursue holiness that leads to a freedom we've never known;
- personally enjoy the intimacy of God's presence;
- participate in the Holy Spirit's transforming work in our lives; and
- prize Jesus above all else.

Word + Spirit

At the end of each day we will respond to a Word + Spirit journal prompt, acknowledging that both God's Word and His Spirit are essential to a deeper, more intimate life with Him. I will ask you to consider what the Holy Spirit is stirring in you or speaking to you each day, so I want to say this: If this practice is unfamiliar to you, or maybe even sounds strange to you, that's okay! It's more than okay. Don't force it, but I beg you to be open to it. This is a process! We are doing this devotional together to *learn* this practice, and I'm hopeful that at the culmination of our forty days, it will feel comfortable and even desirable. I will also be giving you tools as we go for how we can assess if what we are sensing from the Holy Spirit actually *is* the Holy Spirit. We will always test what we *sense* with what the Word *says*!

And finally, at the conclusion of our forty days together, hopefully we will have not only *memorized* our key passage with our minds, but we will *mean* it with our whole hearts. Oh, Lord Jesus, let it be so!

Are you ready to go deeper into the enjoyment of His presence? Me too! Let's do this.

DAY 1

Why Can I Experience Intimacy with God?

I'm guessing the question we each come asking is likely not *why* we can experience intimacy with God but *how*. We want to know *how* to have a vibrant and deeper life with God. We want to know *how* our daily lives can be filled with a sense of His withness. These are such good questions that we are about to answer. But before we answer *how*, we need to appreciate *why*.

Why can we experience intimacy with God the Father? God the Son! Jesus is why!

Without the life, death, resurrection, and ascension of Jesus, we would still be "enemies" of God,[a] deserving wrath, spiritually dead in our sin. Not only would we not be invited into intimate relationship with God, we would have *no* relationship with God at all.

The apostle Paul doesn't dance around this truth when he writes,

> As it is written: "None is righteous, no, not one."
>
> Romans 3:10

I'm giving the bad news first. (Not the smartest way to start a devotional I want you to finish, but stay with me. It gets really good!) Not

a. Romans 5:10 reference.

a single one of us is righteous on our own merit. Show me the most saintly person you know—still not righteous enough to experience relationship with God.

Sin, which means "to miss the mark" through our deliberate decision to disregard God's perfect standard of holiness, created separation from God. Broken relationship caused by our rebellion.

Paul continues, ultimately giving the Good News:

> For the wages of sin is death, but the free gift of God is eternal life in Christ Jesus our Lord.
>
> Romans 6:23

> For everyone who calls on the name of the Lord will be saved!
>
> Romans 10:13

Jesus literally means "God saves." God gives us eternal salvation through His Son, Jesus. And when we receive this gift through faith, we get to enjoy an intimate relationship with Him today!

A.W. Tozer wrote, "What comes into our minds when we think about God is the most important thing about us."[1] And I'd agree. But I'd also encourage us to take it a step further and consider this question: What comes into our minds when we think about the most important things about us? That's what got me thinking about the way we introduce ourselves. For example, when we meet someone new, we tend to share the essentials first. Maybe we say where we live or what we enjoy doing or how we make a living. Maybe we share about our spouse and kids. But if being a child of the King is the most important thing, how do I weave that into the introduction without putting an abrupt end to it? You know what I mean!

Well, I decided to try it out at a women's retreat when it was my turn to introduce myself to the group. I started with what feels like the most important thing. "My name is Jeannie, and I am a daughter of King Jesus." Then I continued with the details one would expect. "I've been married to my husband, Mike, for twenty years, and we have five boys who range from seven to twenty-seven. Our eldest son grew up in an orphanage in Haiti, a place we visit annually that holds a very special place in our hearts. We also have a Golden Retriever named Buddy, who doesn't retrieve but does bring us so much life."

Introducing myself as someone who is loved by Jesus felt right. Yes, I was in a group of women who also know they are loved by Jesus, so it was "safe," but the truth is, belonging to Him is the best and most important thing about me.

I don't say that because I have a particularly intriguing testimony of rescue. I just know that each one of us, no matter how little or much we have strayed from God's holy standard, is doomed without Him. We'd have to face the bleak and difficult realities of this broken world without His strength, comfort, hope, joy, and love. And we'd have no hope of heaven.

Believing that belonging to Jesus is the best thing about us happens when we are honest about the depth of our depravity, who we are without the righteous covering of Christ, and where we'd be if Jesus hadn't rescued us from the path of destruction.

Jesus, now and for eternity, gives us life and peace. And it's unlikely we will ever be compelled to "count everything as loss" compared with the worth of knowing Jesus—as Paul proclaims in our key passage—unless His sacrifice for us becomes so real to us that it wrecks us, in the most beautiful way.

Jesus, now and for eternity, gives us life and peace.

Jesus took the brunt of our sin. He was crucified on the cross, His sinless life given so that we might not only have eternal life but also enjoy personal, intimate relationship with Him on this side of heaven.

When relationships go awry because a person in that relationship messed up, who would we expect to make it right? We typically expect the offender to take action to restore the relationship.

When it comes to our relationship with God, we are the ones who messed it up. Sin entered the world in the Garden of Eden and severed the relationship. And there was nothing we could do to restore it. No résumé of good deeds and generous living was long enough to bridge the gap between His holiness and our unholiness. Between His perfection and our imperfection.

Well, actually, it isn't accurate to say there is *no thing* we can do. There is *one* thing. And it's actually the *only* thing.

The apostle Paul tells us what that is:

> But because of his great love for us, God, who is rich in mercy, made us alive with Christ even when we were dead in transgressions—it is by grace you have been saved. And God raised us up with Christ and seated us with him in the heavenly realms in Christ Jesus, in order that in the coming ages he might show the incomparable riches of his grace, expressed in his kindness to us in Christ Jesus. For it is by grace you have been saved, through faith—and this is not from yourselves, it is the gift of God—not by works, so that no one can boast.
>
> Ephesians 2:4–9 NIV

While we were still spiritually dead in our sin, God, the offended, sent Jesus to reconcile us to himself and restore the broken relationship. It's entirely because of Jesus that we can have intimate relationship with God.

So the one thing we *can* do is receive, by grace through faith, the free gift of salvation in Jesus Christ. When we accept this gift, Christ's righteousness becomes ours. Instantly and eternally.

Fully God and fully man, Jesus lived a sinless life and suffered a brutal death to pay the price for our rebellion and sin. But on the third day, He did just as He said He would do. He defeated death and rose again (oh yes, this is the power of His resurrection Paul talks about in our key passage!), reconciling us to God and closing the divide between our unrighteousness and God's righteousness.

Intimacy with the Trinity (God the Father, God the Son, and God the Holy Spirit) is a free gift given to every person who puts their trust in the finished work of Christ.

Jesus, whose name is above every other name, deserves our wholehearted adoration and praise.

We choose whom, or what, we will worship on this side of heaven. Will it be Him? The One who made a way for us to have a life-altering and loving relationship with God. The One in whom every longing of the human heart is fulfilled. *The One in whom "all the promises of God find their Yes" (2 Corinthians 1:20)!* One day every knee will bow to His authority. One day every mouth will confess His lordship. And one day, when He returns, He will make everything exactly as it was meant to be.

Until then, we have been invited into intimacy *with* the Father through Christ's perfect obedience *to* the Father. Jesus did it all. He loves you that much. He desires relationship with you that deeply.

I pray that sincere gratitude so saturates our hearts that we are compelled to give Him complete access to our lives in the days ahead. May we invite Him to have His way in us so that we may know God's abiding presence in us.

WORD

For further study, read 2 Corinthians 1:20–22. Notice how Paul addresses the essentiality of each member in the Trinity in our salvation. Journal your observations below.

SPIRIT

What do you sense the Holy Spirit stirring in you from your reading today? Pray and invite Him to increase your gratitude for the righteousness that comes from faith in Christ alone!

DAY 2

How Can I Experience Intimacy with God?

I'm going to get right to the point. I hope it doesn't sound too abrupt, but it matters too much. Here it is: A deeply close relationship with God, one in which you enjoy His withness and are sustained by His strength, is something the enemy of your soul is wholeheartedly committed to seeing you forgo. It's true. Of all the things the enemy does not want you to experience (and there are a lot!), intimacy with God is at the top of the list. It's *that* significant in your life of faith!

If we have an enemy actively working against our knowing God's withness, we need to be clear on *how* we pursue and enjoy Him! The answer to how is the Holy Spirit! The work of the Holy Spirit is to ensure you know to whom you belong and to help you enjoy the benefits of this belonging! We get to live in intimate relationship with God the Father because of God the Son through God the Spirit.

The Good News doesn't end at Jesus' death and resurrection that reconciled us to God.

Forty days after His resurrection, Jesus ascended to the Father. But before He left, He said this:

> And I will ask the Father, and he will give you another Helper, to be with you forever, even the Spirit of truth, whom the world cannot receive,

> because it neither sees him nor knows him. You know him, for he dwells with you and will be in you.
>
> John 14:16–17

Sure enough, Jesus did as He promised. He always does. Ten days after His ascension, He sent His Spirit, not only to dwell *with* us, but to live *in* us.

Something that often gets overlooked and undervalued is that Jesus, during His ministry on earth, had the full power of His Spirit in Him. And then, after He ascended to the Father, He sent that same Spirit to live in and operate through us! The same Spirit who filled Jesus fills you and me today. Come on, that's wild! But true. How does this happen? When we put our trust in Jesus, God places His Spirit in us to help us live in confidence of everything that is ours in Jesus.

As Paul explains,

> He redeemed us in order that the blessing given to Abraham might come to the Gentiles through Christ Jesus, so that by faith we might receive the promise of the Spirit.
>
> Galatians 3:14 NIV

The truth that we, by faith, "receive the promise of the Spirit" when we put our trust in Jesus is the part of the salvation narrative that isn't always told. And I don't believe this oversight is intentional. At least, not usually.

For example, we've all seen how athletes write Bible verses on their bodies to tell people about the gospel. In 2009, Tim Tebow wrote John 3:16 on his cheek during the BCS National Championship game, making it the most popular search term for more than twenty-four hours. And I think that's amazing. Yes, get out there and make your face a billboard for His grace! But can we consider putting John 3:16 on the left cheek *and* Acts 2:38 on the right cheek? Too much? That way, after someone Googles John 3:16 and reads, "For God so loved the world, that he gave his only Son, that whoever believes in him should not perish but have eternal life," they'll Google Acts 2:38 and read, "Repent and be baptized every one of you in the name of Jesus Christ for the forgiveness of your sins, and you will receive the gift of the Holy Spirit."

Or athletes could put 1 Corinthians 3:16 on their right cheek: "Do you not know that you are God's temple and that God's Spirit dwells in you?" Or Romans 8:11, "If the Spirit of him who raised Jesus from the dead dwells in you, he who raised Christ Jesus from the dead will also give life to your mortal bodies through his Spirit who dwells in you."

Any of these will do! The point is this: With the free gift of our eternal salvation comes the free gift of the indwelling power of God. They are inseparable. A package deal.

So yes, use your face or your car bumper or your IG profile to make much of Jesus. But don't forget the free gift of enjoying the personal presence and power of God today!

We freely receive salvation *and* the Spirit. New birth. New life. New creation in Christ. The old has gone. The new has come.[a] We are now Spirit-people. Filled with the Spirit. Led by the Spirit. Empowered by the Spirit. Transformed by the Spirit.

But if we don't know this to be true, we keep living as self-people. Filled with the all-sufficient Spirit but led by the insufficient self. Fueled by the flesh. Exhausted and unchanged.

We cannot live like Christ without the power of Christ. Hold on. Read that again. We have no shot at living in our new identities as Spirit-people without the Spirit's power. And we cannot enjoy the deeply personal, tender, and powerful presence of God without welcoming the Spirit of Christ.

If you have put your faith in Jesus, you are home to the Holy Spirit! But let's be honest; a lot of us are a little nervous about making Him feel welcome in His own home. Let's talk about why that's so.

Have you ever made an assumption about somebody you didn't know? Maybe the assumption was based on what you heard about them through a mutual friend. Or maybe it was based on something you read

a. 2 Corinthians 5:17 reference.

about them. Or maybe it was just based on how you'd observed them from afar.

We've all done it. And we often do it with people who intimidate us or people who feel inaccessible to us or who seem to hold more influence or power than we do.

And sometimes our assumptions prove to be correct once we spend time with that person. But oftentimes we discover a person we can appreciate or maybe even enjoy. Once we find ourselves in a conversation with the person we pass in the hallway at church, or the parent we only encounter during the school pickup rush, or the woman we've only known through a filtered life on Instagram, or that neighbor who we've only driven past, or that co-worker we've only emailed with, we discover a lot of our assumptions were unfair or unreasonable. We realize that our opinion of that person was unsubstantiated.

Maybe this is what some of us have done with the Holy Spirit. We've made assumptions about who He is, what He does, and how He'll influence us based on what we've heard about Him or how we've seen things done in His name (things that are not actually *of* Him). Or maybe we've made assumptions about Him not because of what we *have* heard but because of what we *haven't*. How are we to know the significance of His role if we haven't been told?

So our goal, for the next couple days, will be to get to know the Holy Spirit better and assess the assumptions we've held about Him because deep intimacy with God is difficult if we don't trust His Spirit. We can read all the devotions we want, but they won't make much difference without welcoming the work of the Spirit, the One whom Jesus himself called "another Helper . . . the Spirit of Truth." The Holy Spirit makes our relationship with God vibrant, alive, and dynamic. And this kind of relationship is available to every person who calls on the name of Jesus to be saved!

WORD

For further study, read John 16:4–15. Pay attention to verse 7 and journal your thoughts on why Jesus said sending the Holy Spirit would be "to your advantage," or "for your good" (NIV).

SPIRIT

What is the Holy Spirit stirring in you from your reading today? Pray, and invite Him to increase your openness to His role in your life. If you're hesitant, maybe pray, "Make me willing to be willing." He doesn't condemn you for your concerns. He knows how His name has been maligned, how His power has been abused, and how His essential role has been ignored. But perhaps today is the day we begin to move from being led by assumptions about Him to being empowered by a personal experience of Him.

DAY 3

Who Is the Holy Spirit?

Because we tend to think of a person as someone with body parts—head and shoulders, knees and toes—it might feel strange or difficult to say, "the person of Holy Spirit."

But a Biblical definition of personhood isn't the same as the children's song. Biblical personhood means one with an intellect, emotions, and the ability to make decisions. It means you can do relational things, and we undoubtedly see these relational characteristics in all three persons in the Trinity. Yes, even in the Holy Spirit.

So let's get to know Him as a Person—it's important!

God eternally exists as three distinct yet inseparable persons: Father, Son, and Holy Spirit. There is one God, and each person in the Trinity is *fully* God. This means the Holy Spirit is fully God.

My son Finn, who is seven, recently pressed me on this after we read a chapter in *The Jesus Storybook Bible*. "Mom, you've always said there is only one true God. But if God is God, and Jesus is God, and the Holy Spirit is God, then that means there are three gods." Maybe, even as adults, we can identify with Finn's struggle to comprehend the complexity of the Trinity. But as I explained to Finn, while it is a mystery, the more we read Scripture, the better we'll see the Trinity's unity. One God in three persons.

The Holy Spirit is called the third person of the Trinity because He proceeds from the Father and Son. Third person in procession does not mean third place in priority. Third does not mean He is subordinate or less important. He is equal in value and equally essential in the believer's life, and any attempt to live in the *abundance* of God requires *all* of God. *All* being Father, Son, and Holy Spirit.

Scripture refers to the Spirit in a variety of ways—"the Spirit of God," "The Spirit of the LORD," "the Holy Spirit," "the Spirit of holiness," "the Spirit," and "the Spirit of Christ."[a] When you see any of these descriptions, they are all talking about the same divine Person. The Holy Spirit.

God the Father, God the Son, and God the Spirit coexist as the eternal (no beginning and no end), omnipresent (existing everywhere at all times), omniscient (knowing everything), omnipotent (all-powerful), Godhead. Throughout Scripture, we see the trinitarian nature of God on full display!

There are a million other things I want to say about this, but we must keep going. Consider this the CliffsNotes description (and refer to my previous book, *Don't Miss Out*, for a thorough dive into who the Holy Spirit is, what the Holy Spirit does, and why it matters so much!).

It's probably also helpful to address how we might think of the Holy Spirit as an object or a force because these are ways He is symbolized in Scripture. To name a few instances, we see Him descend as a dove at Jesus' baptism in Mark 1:10 and flickering over people's heads as fire on the day of Pentecost in Acts 2:2–3. Also, Jesus describes Him as a flowing river in John 7:37–39 and compares Him to the wind in John 3:8.

While all these symbols carry significance and help us understand how the Spirit works in our world and our lives, He isn't an *it*. He is a divine and indispensable Person of the Trinity. And though His form is not physical, His friendship is experiential.

The more we get to know Him, getting our facts straight from Scripture, I think we'll be stunned that we get to call Him our friend and we'll want to invest a great deal into the relationship! We will only want more of this Person. So let's talk specifics.

a. Genesis 1:2; Exodus 31:3; Judges 3:10; Matthew 1:18; Romans 1:4; Galatians 5:22–23; Ephesians 4:30; 1 Peter 1:11.

He Has a Mind

The Holy Spirit has a brilliant mind. So brilliant we can't grasp it. Paul explains,

> "What no eye has seen, nor ear heard,
> nor the heart of man imagined,
> what God has prepared for those who love him"—
>
> these things God has revealed to us through the Spirit. For the Spirit searches everything, even the depths of God. For who knows a person's thoughts except the spirit of that person, which is in him? So also no one comprehends the thoughts of God except the Spirit of God. Now we have received not the spirit of the world, but the Spirit who is from God, that we might understand the things freely given us by God. And we impart this in words not taught by human wisdom but taught by the Spirit, interpreting spiritual truths to those who are spiritual.
>
> 1 Corinthians 2:9–13

We can't read one another's minds—usually a good thing, right? But there are those times when you've probably had someone, with whom you're having a misunderstanding, say, "I can't read your mind! How was I supposed to know?" That's when it would be helpful to be a mind reader. Otherwise, I think we'd agree it's better that our thoughts are only ours! But it's different with God. Though no one can know God's thoughts except God's Spirit, the Spirit doesn't keep all those to himself. He shares with us! The "mind of the Spirit"—as described in Romans 8:27—searches and dives into the deep things of God and returns to the surface, so to speak, to reveal glorious things to us! What God has done for us, and the inconceivable goodness He has in mind for us, are revealed to us by the Spirit! Are we leaning in and listening?

He Has Feelings

The Holy Spirit is not just a deep thinker. He's a deep feeler. And He stirs up sincere feelings for God in us! And to clarify, this is radically different than the insincere emotionalism that is sometimes attached to Him.

There are many examples in Scripture of the Spirit having feelings. I'll give just a few. In Romans 15:30, Paul appeals to fellow believers "by the love of the Spirit." In Hebrews 10:26–29, we learn the Spirit is "outraged" when we use grace as a license for sin. And in Ephesians 4:30, Paul explains how we bring *grief* to the Holy Spirit when He must co-exist with our intentional sin. His feelings are about our flourishing and the fame of God's name.

He Has a Will

And finally, the Holy Spirit is a decision-maker. He has a will and makes choices on our behalf. For example, did you know that your spiritual gifts were chosen specifically for you by Him? It's not random that you shine where you do. Your spiritual gifts were given to you by the Spirit of God. He decides who gets what, and when.[b]

Further examples include Acts 15:28, where Paul explains how "it seemed good to the Holy Spirit" to make decisions on the people's behalf. Again in Acts 16:6–7, Paul shows us how the Holy Spirit directs us, keeping us from territory that isn't ours to occupy.

The Spirit's Role in Relationship

Not only does the Holy Spirit have relational characteristics, but He is the One who makes our relationship with God so deeply personal and intimate. He is the personal presence of God in us. He is the person of the Trinity by whom we experience God so intimately.

This is the heart of Paul's teaching in Ephesians 3:14–21:

> For this reason I bow my knees before the Father, from whom every family in heaven and on earth is named, that according to the riches of

b. 1 Corinthians 12:11 reference.

> his glory he may grant you to be strengthened with power through his Spirit in your inner being, so that Christ may dwell in your hearts through faith—that you, being rooted and grounded in love, may have strength to comprehend with all the saints what is the breadth and length and height and depth, and to know the love of Christ that surpasses knowledge, that you may be filled with all the fullness of God.
>
> Now to him who is able to do far more abundantly than all that we ask or think, according to the power at work within us, to him be glory in the church and in Christ Jesus throughout all generations, forever and ever. Amen.

Paul prays that we may be strengthened with what? Power. How? Through the Holy Spirit! Where? In our inner man. In our spirit. Why? That we would comprehend the incomprehensible love of Jesus and be filled with the fullness of God!

Intimacy with God is the goal, and it is entirely possible for every person in whom Christ dwells. The Holy Spirit strengthens us with power to have more than head knowledge of God's love. He makes it real in our inner being, bringing intimacy into our relationship with our triune God.

The doctrine of the Trinity is essential to our understanding and enjoying intimacy with God! What a gift we've been given in Him!

WORD

For further study, reread Ephesians 3:14–21. But this time, pay particular attention to the last sentence. Notice what God is able to do by the Spirit's power at work within us, "far more abundantly" than we can imagine!

SPIRIT

Which relational characteristic(s) of the Holy Spirit stood out to you or surprised you most? Why? Journal your thoughts below and pay attention in the days ahead to these aspects of His personhood.

DAY 4

What Does Pentecost Mean for Me?

My husband, Mike, and I were introduced by mutual friends. When they set us up, Mike was living in New York City, and I had just moved to Washington, D.C. Until we were married about eighteen months later, we were in a long-distance relationship. We logged countless hours on the phone and though we learned a whole lot about each other in those long conversations, I counted down the days until we were back in each other's presence. You may not have been in a long-distance romantic relationship, but all of us have long-distance relationships with family or friends. And we know that while the relationship can be sustained by communication, it is strengthened in one another's presence. There is intimacy in close proximity that isn't experienced at a distance.

Do you know who does *not* want to be in a long-distance relationship with you? Jesus.[1] How do I know? The day of Pentecost. Pentecost is the proof that Jesus is about presence.

Pentecost is the monumental day that the church was birthed, that Christ's power inhabited His people, and that the gospel began to spread like wildfire—so why do we rarely hear about it from the pulpit?

Christmas, the day we celebrate the birth of Christ.

Easter, the day we celebrate the resurrection of Christ.

Pentecost, the day we celebrate the indwelling power of Christ, the day God's omnipresence became His indwelling presence and manifest presence!

On Pentecost God poured the Holy Spirit *into* His people, ushering in an experience of unforeseen supernatural power that continues to defy human understanding and supersede human strength.

A little history: Pentecost occurred fifty days after Jesus' resurrection (this fifty days includes forty days after his resurrection and ten days after His ascension into heaven). At 9:00 a.m., the Father unleashed the Holy Spirit in the upper room where 120 people, including the disciples, were praying and waiting to be filled with God, just as Jesus had told them to do.

The story unfolded in the most dramatic way!

> When the day of Pentecost arrived, they were all together in one place. And suddenly there came from heaven a sound like a mighty rushing wind, and it filled the entire house where they were sitting. And divided tongues as of fire appeared to them and rested on each one of them. And they were all filled with the Holy Spirit and began to speak in other tongues as the Spirit gave them utterance.
>
> Acts 2:1–4

There was nothing subtle about God sending the Holy Spirit. A mighty wind rushed through the room. Tongues of fire flickered over their heads. Then the men and women began speaking in a number of different languages. "Other tongues" means they were empowered to speak known and recognizable languages they had not previously known how to speak, but languages that *were* recognizable to Jews who had come from other nations. Imagine you've traveled to a country where you don't speak the native language, but suddenly you can understand what they're saying. It's not that you learned their language. It's that God enabled them to speak yours. That's what happened at Pentecost for Jews who had traveled there.

God was so intentional in His timing. The Holy Spirit descended on a day when devout Jews from every nation gathered in Jerusalem. And when the God-fearing Jews heard the commotion in the upper room, they came running to see what was happening. In doing so, they were all able to hear the gospel being preached in their own language and bore witness to the mighty work of the Holy Spirit.[a]

The gospel was no longer bound by language or ethnic barriers. The church was birthed! The triune God ordained it and enabled it! But not everyone who witnessed it believed it or liked it. They couldn't help but have a strong reaction—one not too different than many people probably would have today!

> "They are speaking of the powerful works of God to all of us in our own language! . . . What can this mean?" But others laughed and made fun, saying, "These men are full of new wine."
>
> Acts 2:11–13 NLV

But Scripture tells us they weren't overindulging in pinot noir; they were overcome with the Spirit of God. They weren't about to be lying in bed with a hangover. They were about to light the world ablaze with the hope of Christ. The Good News!

"This is a great story, but what does this mean for me today?" you might be asking.

It means that all this, and more, is ours to experience and enjoy today! On the day of Pentecost lives were instantly and dramatically transformed. Supernatural power and love broke through. Faith increased. Joy exploded. Courage multiplied. The power that Jesus said would allow us to do even greater works than He did began to break out.[b]

If Pentecost had not occurred, and God had not fulfilled the promise Jesus made to His disciples to send His Spirit, we would be living within our human limitations, dependent upon our strength alone to navigate the harsh realities of this fallen world. We wouldn't know or enjoy the

a. Acts 2:5–11 reference.
b. John 14:12 reference.

manifest presence of God that became a reality for all Jesus' followers on Pentecost. We would (rightfully) fear that the Holy Spirit could depart from us, and that His anointing on our lives was temporary, as it was for people in the Old Testament who had His empowering for a specific task but couldn't count on it to remain. We wouldn't have intimacy with Jesus that leads to spiritual and emotional healing, physical healing, relational healing, and true and lasting transformation.

Without Pentecost, we would see our struggles through the filter of our own capacity rather than faith in His capacity. But because the Holy Spirit lives in us, we carry His capacity. Think about that! You carry God's capacity! What feels too big for you to overcome? What feels too heavy to carry? Speak the name Jesus—and the power of His resurrection—over those things.

Because of Pentecost, we get to (get to!!) do life with Jesus indwelling us by His Spirit. His capacity is uncontainable.

> Because of Pentecost, we get to do life with Jesus indwelling us by His Spirit. His capacity is uncontainable.

The Holy Spirit manifests His power in followers of Jesus who welcome Him and make themselves available.

The book of Acts is an extraordinary testament to what happens when people yield themselves as conduits of God's power. That's what the disciples did after they were filled by God's personal presence. They availed themselves of His purposes. And they always gave God the praise for what was accomplished in His name.

You and I are also meant to be conduits of God's power, sparking curiosity about Jesus in a world desperate to encounter His transforming love. This can happen in small ways every day, simply by sharing our stories of forgiveness, hope, healing, and transformation. By not being silent about the gospel and the surpassing worth of knowing Jesus with someone who has yet to meet Him. By asking a friend how you can pray and believing your prayer has power. By humbly meeting needs around you, serving as the hands and feet of Jesus. By living generously because He's been so generous to you, and because it all belongs to Him anyhow.

Will it cost you your comfort? Probably. Is He worth it? Absolutely. I can't help but think that the greater cost is missing out on living lives availed to His purposes, and meandering our way through a life void of meaning and eternal impact. Not only are we missing out on experiencing what only God can do *in* us, but others won't experience Him *through* us.

Everything God did through His people who were indwelt by His power in the New Testament is ours to experience and enjoy today. We can hear Him speak, we can be led by His Spirit, we can live in His power, we can grow in His likeness, we can fulfill our God-ordained purpose, all by His indwelling Spirit, and all to make much of His greatness.

WORD

For further study, read John 14:5–14, where Jesus is teaching His disciples that they will do even greater things than He did because these are works done in the power of the Holy Spirit. If this is just as true for us as it was for them, what does this mean for you today? Journal your thoughts below.

SPIRIT

Pray and ask the Holy Spirit to increase your capacity for Him and to help you rely on His capacity in you, to heighten your awareness of His presence in you. Thank Him for making His home in you, for giving you everything that is yours in Jesus, and for what He has prepared to show you and to do in you as we seek a deeper life with God over these forty days.

DAY 5

Does God Manifest Himself in Me?

I take great comfort in knowing God is omnipresent, meaning He is everywhere present, though I'll admit it's impossible to comprehend. How is He right here with me as I type this sentence and also beyond the galaxies the Hubble telescope is able to probe? How is it that God is present in His creation but not contained by it? Indeed, He is above and beyond all we see and know. He is, always has been and always will be, present in every place, all the time. He even dwells within me by His Spirit. Yes, God's abiding presence with His people is the main storyline of Scripture.

So with the Psalmist we gladly can say,

> Where shall I go from your Spirit?
> Or where shall I flee from your presence?
> If I ascend to heaven, you are there!
> If I make my bed in Sheol, you are there!
> If I take the wings of the morning
> and dwell in the uttermost parts of the sea,
> even there your hand shall lead me,
> and your right hand shall hold me.
>
> Psalm 139:7–10

If we know God's heart toward us, this feels like good news. Really good news. But if we don't know God's heart toward us, this can feel like bad news, as demonstrated by an image I saw on a young woman's hoodie.

It was a picture of Jesus in a long white robe, peeking His head out from behind a wall, with a disapproving look on His face and a word bubble above His head that read, "I saw that!" I'll admit, I laughed at first, but then sadness washed over me because the message was clear: Jesus is the creepy spy guy, always watching and waiting to catch you messing up.

That's not Jesus.

Yes, Jesus is always present and always watching, but as the well-known hymn "His Eye Is on the Sparrow" reminds us, His presence is not creepy. It's our confidence!

> A constant Friend is He:
> His eye is on the sparrow,
> And I know He watches me; . . .
>
> I sing because I'm happy,
> I sing because I'm free,
> For His eye is on the sparrow,
> And I know He watches me.[1]

Though our awareness of His withness will not always be obvious or felt, we can have confidence because nothing goes unnoticed with Jesus.

But what about God's manifest presence? How is that different from God's omnipresence and indwelling presence?

Because the word *manifest* carries different meanings to different people, I think it's important to clarify what *we* mean by God's manifest presence. Most important, we need to know we don't manifest God. We aren't capable of coercing or forcing God to make himself known or felt. When someone says they manifest something in their lives, that "thing" is never anything of God because He chooses how, when, and where He reveals himself or produces His character and power through us.

His manifest presence means it is "clear or obvious to the eye or mind."[2] It is the experienced or known presence of God. And because the Bible emphasizes the manifest presence of God as essential to our relationship with Him, we cannot ignore it. And why would we want to? Why would we want to pass up the precious invitation to be in God's relational presence? The same presence that led David to declare in Psalm 16:11, "in your presence there is fullness of joy; at your right hand are pleasures forevermore!" Isn't that what we're all searching for? It's found in His presence!

Because the Bible emphasizes the manifest presence of God as essential to our relationship with Him, we cannot ignore it. And why would we want to?

Maybe this example can be helpful in thinking about the difference. It's not uncommon for children to have a fear of the dark. Or just a fear of the night. How many of us have lost a good night's sleep to a child who climbed into our bed to be comforted in their nighttime fear? How many of us have been awakened by a kick to the ribs or an arm flung into our face by a child who just needed to know we're near as they sleep?

One of our boys went through a season like this. And on one particular night, when his 1:00 a.m. visit woke me abruptly, I launched into a lecture on how he can't keep coming into our room, how he needs to learn to trust that he is safe in our house because we are there, and how he doesn't have to be right next to us to trust this is true. It wasn't my finest moment.

The next morning, however, as I intentionally sought the Lord's presence because I needed more than just the knowledge of His existence, the Lord brought me back to the situation with my son the night before. (This is an example of how the Holy Spirit communicates with us. He "speaks" to us with thoughts that are not our own.)

The Lord showed me how my son's knowing we are present in the house feels different than drawing near to our presence. Feeling our arms around him and hearing our breath beside him is different than knowing we exist inside these walls when he's afraid. I went straight to my son to seek his forgiveness for my harshness and I shared how I often feel the same way with God! (I also told him he still needs to work on staying in bed!)

This is a bit like knowing God is omnipresent versus knowing His manifest presence.

The idea of experiencing His presence, through hearing His voice, sensing His withness, or seeing His hand at work, might sound impossible or extreme to some. And I understand why. If the eyes of your heart have not been opened by the Holy Spirit to the beauty and majesty of God's love given freely in Jesus Christ, you wouldn't expect God to give himself so freely to you in such relational and intimate ways. When we remember that Paul wrote "The god of this age [the devil] has blinded the minds of unbelievers, so that they cannot see the light of the gospel that displays the glory of Christ, who is the image of God" (2 Corinthians 4:4 NIV), we can better understand why encountering God doesn't add up for unbelieving hearts.

So let's circle back to the doctrine of the Trinity for a moment to remember how this happens.

The eternal triune God reveals himself to us as Father, Son, and Holy Spirit with distinct personal attributes, but without division of nature, essence, or being. The trinitarian structure appears throughout the New Testament to affirm that God himself is manifested through Jesus Christ by means of the Spirit.

The Spirit's presence is the manifestation of the Trinity among us today. Meaning, whenever you sense God's presence, you are sensing the work of the Holy Spirit! And though He carries the same authority and shares the same attributes as God the Father and God the Son, He performs distinct functions. This is important and speaks to the tragedy of the Spirit often being neglected and forgotten. God the Holy Spirit does specific work in us that differs from that of God the Father and God the Son.

So we need to welcome the work of the Holy Spirit *if* we want to receive all that is ours in Jesus and experience God's manifest presence.

If we have misconceptions about the Holy Spirit, or if we fear He is weird, or that He'll make us weird, or that He's an optional extra for extra-Christians, we will quench Him. And when we quench God's Spirit with our fear, pride, need to control, or just neglect, we miss God's manifest presence that makes all the difference in our lives.

So, though we cannot force God to manifest himself, making His love known and His presence felt, we *do* know God loves to do this. He desires for you to experience His love! To go deeper into love. The more aware we are of His manifest presence, the more we will live in awe and healthy fear of Him. The more overwhelmed we are by His loving presence, the more we will walk in obedience to His Word because we won't want to do anything to diminish this priceless gift.

This is what He wants for each of us. "To know Him and the power of His resurrection!" Having our hearts open to and aware of God and His presence can bring vibrancy to the most tedious and commonplace parts of our day. What a miraculous gift that we, as people who have put their trust in Jesus, get to experience His loving presence through His Spirit!

WORD

For further study, read Psalm 73:23–28. Reflect on verse 28. The CSB translation reads, "But as for me, God's presence is my good." The ESV reads, "But for me it is good to be near God." What does this mean for you today? Journal your thoughts.

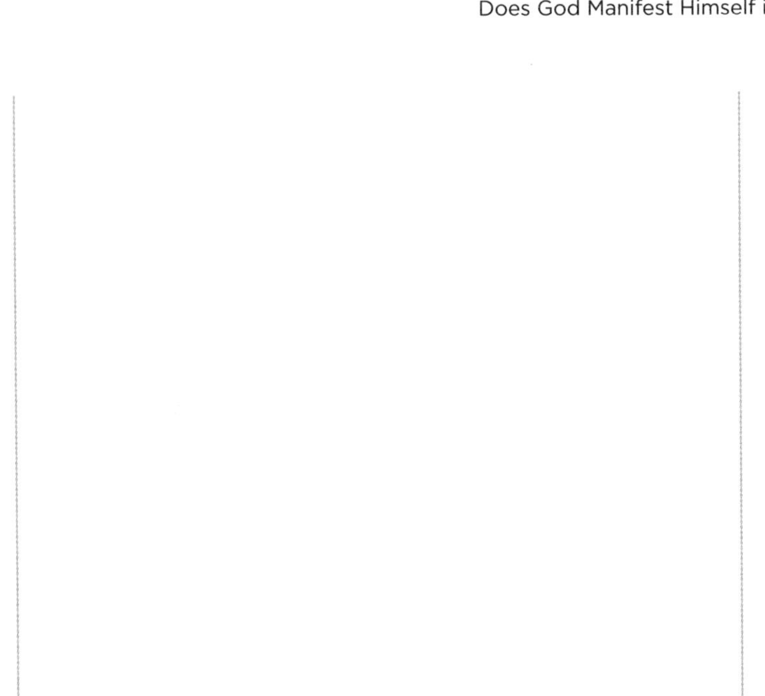

SPIRIT

Pray and ask the Holy Spirit to open your eyes to His hand at work all around you, to open your ears to hear Him speaking to you, to open your senses to His presence enfolding you. Visualize yourself leaning back against God's chest, embraced in His arms of love. Invite Him to make himself known.

DAY 6

How Do I Miss Out on God's Manifest Presence?

Something I've discovered through conversations with other Christians is that it's easier for us to say, "God is everywhere" than it is for us to say, "God is here," or even "God is here *in me*." And the reason primarily seems to be that acknowledging His personal presence requires a response. God "out there somewhere" isn't personal and intimate, so it's easier to ignore Him, especially when we aren't living a life that honors Him.

But when we acknowledge we are carriers of His presence, and that the way God manifests His presence is by His Holy Spirit in us, we must decide what we'll do about that. Will we ignore Him, or will we invite Him to have His way?

God's manifest presence isn't a new thing. Just because the word *manifest* is having a moment in popular culture doesn't mean God's presence is new or momentary. There are countless examples of God's manifest presence in Scripture. His manifest presence was with Adam and Eve when He walked with them in the Garden of Eden. God made himself manifest to Moses in the burning bush in Exodus 3, and to Daniel and his companions in the fiery furnace when they would not worship Nebuchadnezzar's image in Daniel 3:24–25. His presence was manifest in the tabernacle in the Old Testament, in the incarnation of

Christ in John 1:14, and at Pentecost when He inhabited His people by the Holy Spirit.

Each one of these examples demonstrates that His presence always has a purpose. When His presence manifests, our awareness of Him is awakened, and something usually shifts. Burdens are lightened. Hearts are strengthened. Spirits are lifted. Anxious thoughts are calmed. When an aspect of God's character is experienced, we are different for it. Sometimes it's in very small ways on very ordinary days, maybe while we're driving our car having an honest conversation with God, or opening the Word and studying the verse of the day, or taking a walk while listening to music that makes much of Jesus. And sometimes His manifest presence is felt in monumental ways, ways you won't ever forget. How incredibly gracious of our God to allow us to know His presence.

But we can't ignore a simple fact we will return to again and again. Sin impedes our experience of God's manifest presence. We witness this in the beginning of time through Adam and Eve, who become exiles of Eden through their disobedience to God and their disregard for His one command in Genesis 3:3, "You shall not eat of the fruit of the tree that is in the midst of the garden." Satan deceived them with four simple words. "Did God actually say . . . ?" He still does this to us today. He gets us to doubt God's goodness. He gets us to question God's Word and even twist it to justify our choices. And we fall for it, just as Eve did.

Because of their sin, Adam and Eve's eyes were opened to their nakedness, and their ability to freely enjoy God's presence was hindered. But what does God do then? Does He abandon them? I can't imagine we'd blame Him if He did. But instead, He pursues them. He covers their nakedness with garments, just as He covers us with Christ's righteousness. God desires relationship that much. Yet still, communion with God is now broken. But this isn't the end of the story.

Through Christ, God entered into the story. The author wrote himself into the narrative. God, in Christ, took on flesh. He lived in perfect obedience, then died for our disobedience so that we might once again draw near. Draw near to what? His relational presence! He is not distant. He dwells among us. And He sent His Spirit to live in us, permanently uniting us to Christ, and manifesting His power and presence in our lives.

But let us not miss God's goal in all of this. It isn't goosebumps, though we may physically sense when the Holy Spirit fills us afresh, and that's a beautiful thing. I certainly have felt His filling, and it gives me great assurance of His love, but this isn't the ultimate purpose.

For example, I recently had coffee with a friend who asked to get together to discuss some things she felt God was doing in her life. She explained how earlier in the week she'd been reading her Bible, as she typically did, but on this particular day she was moved by the Spirit to a time of repentance. She said that it wasn't like God was revealing some "big new sins" she'd been ignoring or hiding. She just felt led to repent for how she misses the mark in her everyday life. It was a sweet time, she said, and it brought the refreshment and closeness she didn't even realize she was missing. Then, days later, while she was at a worship gathering, worshipers were invited to put out their hands and ask the Holy Spirit for a fresh filling of His presence. And when she did, she felt a physical touch to her hands. An imparting, so to speak, of God's presence and power. She then remembered her time of repentance and felt the assurance that the Lord was responding to her repentance with this gift of filling and physically enjoying His presence. And while her physical experience was beautiful and biblical, it's not the goal. Godliness is.

God's goal is to transform us into the likeness of His Son, like Paul, who prayed to "know him and the power of his resurrection." He allows us to experience His manifest presence so we will know more of His love, His purpose, His holiness, and His transforming power. God wants us to grow in godliness.

When He feels distant, I assess where sin might be hindering His manifest presence. I have to take an honest look at whether I am living in disagreement with the Spirit, or intentionally pursuing sin, or stubbornly holding on to something God is asking me to surrender to Him—therefore forfeiting the benefit of being enveloped in His presence. Is He still with me? Of course. I am sealed with the Spirit and confident He will not abandon me. It's vital that we understand this, as Paul explained it in Ephesians 1:13–14:

> In him you also, when you heard the word of truth, the gospel of your salvation, and believed in him, were sealed with the promised Holy Spirit, who is the guarantee of our inheritance until we acquire possession of it, to the praise of his glory.

We become His permanent dwelling place when we put our trust in Jesus, and He doesn't pack up and put up a For Sale sign when we live in intentional sin. His permanent presence is the guarantee of our inheritance!

Let us know with absolute confidence, God's manifest presence is not predicated on perfect obedience. If it were, none of us would experience God. We sin every single day. If not in deed, then in thought or motive. Sin is first and foremost a matter of the heart.

But we will not experience the fullness of God's presence when we are pursuing sin instead of Him. Our disobedience diminishes our sense of God's presence and causes us to forfeit the ministry of His presence. The joy we experience in God's presence is what wanes when we walk off the path of life. We can't say with our mouths "I want all you have for me!" but live on our own terms. Jesus loves us too much to honor our hypocrisy and lukewarm Christianity.

God's desire is that every believer would enjoy the gift of His manifest presence. For example, when we give special gifts to people we love, we would grieve if they opened the gift, called themselves unworthy of such generosity and extravagance, and stuffed it back in the gift bag. So it is with God giving us His Spirit, who leads us into intimacy with the Trinity.

The Spirit's presence is the manifestation of God's power. It's the manifestation of the character of Christ, the fruit of the Spirit. Love. Joy. Peace. Patience. Kindness. Goodness. Gentleness. Faithfulness. Self-control. The Spirit's (ungrieved) presence produces greater intimacy with God. He fills us afresh so we can experience and produce the effect of His presence. Will we stubbornly pursue self-centered living, settling for less than the enjoyment of His withness, or will we surrender our will to His and live lives filled with His presence to grow in His likeness?

WORD

For further study, open your Bible and read Hebrews 4:16 and record it below. How are we invited to draw near to God? What will we find when we do?

SPIRIT

What do you sense the Holy Spirit stirring in you? Invite Him to bring His loving conviction to you about the things that might be hindering God's manifest presence. Take a moment to draw near to God in prayer now and receive His mercy and grace.

DAY 7

How Does the Spirit Foster Intimacy with God?

To be sure I am not simplifying the Holy Spirit's role to *only* fostering intimacy with God, I want to begin today by looking at how Jesus spoke of the broad—and beautiful—scope of the Spirit's role in our lives.

In John 14:16, Jesus is preparing his disciples for the coming of the Holy Spirit because He knows His crucifixion is imminent. He says,

> I will ask the Father, and he will give you another Helper, to be with you forever.

The disciples were distraught. They didn't understand. "How could Jesus depart from us? Where is He going? We don't want 'another Helper,' we want Jesus!" What the disciples didn't yet comprehend is that this "another Helper" wasn't just *any* helper and He doesn't provide just any ole help. The original Greek word translated "Helper" is *parakletos* and it's so full of meaning that it can be translated as comforter, counselor, advocate, strengthener, intercessor, standby, and champion.

The Holy Spirit, our consummate Helper, guides us, comforts us, fills us with hope and joy, gives us life and peace, strengthens us in our inner being, communicates with us, prays for us, leads us in truth, empowers us to fight sin, illuminates Scripture, and advocates for us. He leads us to a deeper knowledge of gospel truth and gives us supernatural gifts to build up the church and glorify God. And He not only opens our hearts to the love of Jesus and makes us more like Jesus, but He also brings immense intimacy to our relationship with Jesus!

The extent of His activity in our lives goes on and on.

Over the last twenty-four hours, I've found myself in deep conversations with two people I don't usually go deep with, and as I write this devotion today, I realize this was no coincidence. These two people are in very different stages of life, but both of them concluded their descriptions of how they're feeling lately with the same word: *empty*. These two people lead full and successful lives. But still, there is a void, a longing to be filled. It was a good reminder that physical abundance is unlike spiritual aliveness.

There have been many times in my life when I could relate to their feelings of emptiness. I'm certain we all can. It might not be a persistent feeling, but oftentimes, the things we pursue that we expect to fill us disappoint us because they cannot provide what they promise, whether that's a relationship or a level of success or an experience. These things can provide a temporary sense of safety, pleasure, or accomplishment, but they can't fill us. And the more we expect them to fill us, the more likely they are to leave us feeling empty.

This is where the Holy Spirit comes in and does what He was given to do.

Paul explains,

> God's love has been poured out into our hearts through the Holy Spirit, who has been given to us.
>
> Romans 5:5 NIV

The Holy Spirit pours the love of God into the emptiness of our hearts. Don't miss the word *pours*. Imagine a bottomless pitcher, not a leaky faucet. The Spirit of God gives us the love of God in abundance. He is not a God of scarcity but abundance. And it is right and good to pray for an experience of God's love poured into our hearts!

The words "poured out" remind me of the story in John 12 when Jesus went to have dinner with Lazarus (whom He'd raised from the dead!) and his sisters, Mary and Martha. This happened six days before Passover, when Jesus would be crucified for us. Mary, in adoration and love, poured out a jar of expensive aromatic oils onto Jesus' feet, anointing Him for His burial. It was the most costly thing in her life. (A full year of wages kind of costly!) "The house was filled with the fragrance of the perfume," we are told in verse 3.

When the Holy Spirit pours the love of God into our hearts, it is meant to fill the house. You are that house, the temple of God. And this love was more costly than a year's wages. It cost Christ His life. The Spirit wants to fill you with the fullness of God, the beautiful aroma of Christ permeating every room in your heart, influencing everything that flows *from* your heart. Your thoughts, your feelings, your words, your actions. What you think about, what you feel, what you speak.[a]

We have to let our guard down with the Spirit if we want God's love poured in! Because we can say we believe in Jesus, and even have correct theology about the Holy Spirit, but remain resistant to allowing the Spirit to pour God's love into our life. We can remain resistant to intimacy with God. It's not uncommon among professing Christians to know *about* Him and still not *know* Him and His loving presence.

The remedy for feeling distant from God and His love is not usually a better explanation of it but an experience of it. This is what the Holy Spirit makes possible!

For example, we bought a lake house several years ago. It feels like holy ground. Everyone who visits calls it a place of peace, and I'd agree. But there has always been one little thing that I haven't loved about our lake house and that's the poor water pressure in the shower heads. I tried all the things I normally do to increase water pressure, to no avail.

The solution came when I asked our handyman for help. He informed me that our outdoor water pressure is so strong that it burst his pressure cleaner weeks prior. After a little digging, he discovered that the

a. Proverbs 4:23 reference.

water pressure for the property wasn't the problem. The problem was the pressure valve inside the house that was preventing the water from flowing as it should through the home.

Similarly, the availability of God's deeply personal love isn't the problem. The problem is the pressure valve—which we could call our resistance or skepticism or uncertainty or unwillingness—that prevents us from receiving the love that the Spirit pours into our hearts.

It is through the Person of the Holy Spirit that we get to enjoy fellowship with the Father and Son. The Spirit was sent to guide our hearts to adoration and awe of Jesus. The Holy Spirit makes God's love grow from awareness in our head to affection in our heart. He stirs our hearts to call out to God as Abba Father, and He welcomes us into the intimacy of the Trinity that we were made to enjoy.

The Holy Spirit makes God's love grow from awareness in our head to affection in our heart.

The Holy Spirit applies the love that Christ secured. He puts it into full operation in our lives. He makes it real to us. He makes it alive in us.

We experience God in the majestic wonder of His creation (don't take me on a hike to a waterfall and expect me not to experience the glory of God). We experience God when we sing to Him in the kitchen over a sink full of dishes. We experience God when we are creating something. We experience God when we are strengthening our bodies. The list of ways we can experience Him is long, but this is one we might not love: We experience God in our suffering. I was reminded of this in a recent conversation with a widowed mama of seven who shared how her suffering has drawn her into deeper intimacy with God. She wasn't putting a spiritual bow on her pain, but she *was* acknowledging how God has been so very tender and present in it.

I, too, have known the tenderness of His presence in my pain. When I have walked through heart-wrenching things, when I have pounded on His chest and poured out my pain, His love has been my lifeline.

Paul also understood this. More than most, I believe. Think of our key passage in which he wrote (emphasis mine), "that I may know him and the power of his resurrection, ***and may share his sufferings.***" Maybe suffering is where we know Him and His resurrection power most?

The experience of God's love is the supernatural work of the Holy Spirit. And our lives are meant to testify to the lavishness of this love! In fact, when we experience how great this love is, we can't help but become givers of it. Christ's love is compelling. It changes us and compels us to live in a way that says, "His presence makes all the difference!"

It's not too good to be true. His profuse goodness won't be yanked away from you. May His invitation to intimacy never intimidate us. Or as my wise friend Phylicia Masonheimer says, "May His abundance never scare you, and always drive you to love."[1]

WORD

For further study, open your Bible and read Romans 5:1–11 to gain more context for the verse that we read today (Romans 5:5). Record below your thoughts from your reading.

SPIRIT

Invite the Holy Spirit to illuminate where you've sought to fill the emptiness with anything other than Him, and invite the Holy Spirit to fill you with His love and draw you into deeper intimacy with the Lover of your soul.

DAY 8

How Do We See Intimacy Modeled by Jesus?

Jesus is so relational. Throughout the Gospels, we find Him enjoying meals with people (many of whom others shunned), walking and talking with them, pursuing them and welcoming them in. Never do we see Jesus saying, even to the those who were considered the greatest of sinners and the lowliest of outcasts, "Don't get too close. Keep just enough distance between you and me. I'll tell you what to do, but I don't want to be in relationship with you." No, that's not Jesus. He made himself accessible. His earthly ministry is woven with extensive evidence of His desire to be in intimate relationship. We see this in how He interacts with people while He is among them, but we also see this in the sending of His Spirit to live in us when He is no longer physically present.

When we read John chapter 15, we quickly find several statements demonstrating His invitation to intimacy as He teaches on how He is the True Vine, His Father is the Gardener, and we are the branches.

I'd encourage you to read this passage slowly, and out loud. There are ten sermons packed into this one passage, but our goal today is to pay attention to the invitation to union and withness throughout.

> I am the true vine, and my Father is the gardener. He cuts off every branch in me that bears no fruit, while every branch that does bear fruit he prunes

> so that it will be even more fruitful. You are already clean because of the word I have spoken to you. Remain in me, as I also remain in you. No branch can bear fruit by itself; it must remain in the vine. Neither can you bear fruit unless you remain in me.
>
> I am the vine; you are the branches. If you remain in me and I in you, you will bear much fruit; apart from me you can do nothing. If you do not remain in me, you are like a branch that is thrown away and withers; such branches are picked up, thrown into the fire and burned. If you remain in me and my words remain in you, ask whatever you wish, and it will be done for you. This is to my Father's glory, that you bear much fruit, showing yourselves to be my disciples.
>
> As the Father has loved me, so have I loved you. Now remain in my love. If you keep my commands, you will remain in my love, just as I have kept my Father's commands and remain in his love. I have told you this so that my joy may be in you and that your joy may be complete. My command is this: Love each other as I have loved you. Greater love has no one than this: to lay down one's life for one's friends. You are my friends if you do what I command. I no longer call you servants, because a servant does not know his master's business. Instead, I have called you friends, for everything that I learned from my Father I have made known to you. You did not choose me, but I chose you and appointed you so that you might go and bear fruit—fruit that will last—and so that whatever you ask in my name the Father will give you. This is my command: Love each other.
>
> John 15:1–17 NIV

Notice the statements made by Jesus:

"Remain in me, as I also remain in you."

"As the Father has loved me, so I have loved you. Now remain in my love."

"I have told you this so that my joy may be in you and that your joy may be complete."

"Love each other as I have loved you."

"I have called you friends."

"I chose you."

Remain. Stay close. Always connected. Intimacy. His Word inhabiting us! Jesus describes a life of abiding as a life lived in the truth (the Word!) and the love of the Trinity that ultimately compels us to live like Him and love one another.

I have a wooden block on my desk that reads "I love us," and out of the top of that block is a wire hook that holds a picture of my precious family. All seven of us holding on to each other tightly. Oh how I love us!

I often think of the Trinity when I look at the words on that wooden block. If the Trinity had a desk in heaven, I think they'd put that wooden block on it, and there'd be a picture of them in the wire hook. There is unfathomable love that flows between our triune God. And here's the miracle: *We* are invited into that love. Not just invited in but told to stay. To remain.

We see further evidence of our invitation to intimacy in John chapter 17 as Jesus prays for himself, for His disciples, and for us! Jesus, before He became our perfect sacrifice, prayed,

> That they may have the full measure of my joy within them.
>
> John 17:13 NIV

> Righteous Father . . . I have made you known to them, and will continue to make you known in order that the love you have for me may be in them and that I myself may be in them.
>
> John 17:25–27 NIV

Jesus prays for His joy to be *in* us. His love to be *in* us. His Spirit to be *in* us. Not just around us or within reach, but *in* us.

And it is by His Spirit *in us* that we are compelled to respond not as slaves to a master but as sons and daughters to a father!

Paul explains it this way:

> For you did not receive the spirit of slavery to fall back into fear, but you have received the Spirit of adoption as sons, by whom we cry, "Abba! Father!" The Spirit himself bears witness with our spirit that we are

> children of God, and if children, then heirs—heirs of God and fellow heirs with Christ, provided we suffer with him in order that we may also be glorified with him.
>
> Romans 8:15–17

His Spirit beckons us to call God “Abba,” just as Jesus did. *Abba* is the Aramaic word Jesus used for *Father* in the Lord’s prayer, and it’s the word children with an intimate relationship with their father would use. It’s the word that signifies safety, lest we “fall back into fear.” There is no safer place than *in* Him.

I’m grateful that I have always had a very loving and safe relationship with my dad. One that led me to call him Daddy more than any other name. Even as an adult with five children of my own, it feels most natural to call him Daddy. I was reminded how precious this is after listening to a dear friend share, with tear-drenched cheeks, how she always longed to feel close enough to her father to call him Daddy when she was a little girl. That word *Daddy* represented a depth and tenderness that she did not have but desperately wanted. Thankfully, this longing in her heart was satisfied later in life. I loved listening to her share how it was even sweeter than she’d imagined to enter into this relational intimacy with her father.

How sweet it is to know that no matter what complexities our relationships with our earthly fathers hold, our heavenly Father invites us into this kind of relational intimacy with Him. He is our only perfect Father.

We are sons and daughters of God. But not just sons and daughters. Heirs. The inheritance of God is ours because of Jesus. What the wealthiest earthly father might leave for his children does not begin to compare to the inheritance we receive from our heavenly Father. It’s not temporal. It’s eternal.

Jesus made a way for us to have a loving relationship with God. Jesus modeled this loving relationship during His ministry on earth. Jesus prayed that we would experience this loving relationship in our own lives. And the Spirit now makes this loving relationship alive in us.

I want us to be so captivated by Jesus that if we could only ask for one thing from Him, it would echo the psalmist who prays,

> One thing I ask from the LORD,
> this only do I seek:
> that I may dwell in the house of the LORD
> all the days of my life,
> to gaze on the beauty of the LORD
> and to seek him in his temple.
>
> Psalm 27:4 NIV

To seek Him in His temple is to pursue His presence! Though His presence was once confined to the temple, it is now present in us and all around us. To gaze upon Jesus all our days . . . that's the incomparable prize!

WORD

We read a lot of Scripture today, so I'd just ask that you return to John 15 to reflect on, and record below how we are to emulate abiding and intimacy as Jesus modeled for us.

SPIRIT

Pray and pursue God's presence. Be intentional today to abide and remain in His love. Stay awake to God today.

DAY 9

What Determines Depth of Intimacy with God?

I think the best conversations are had while walking. Would you agree? There's just something about walking and talking (with coffee in hand, of course) that breeds good communication. When Mike asks me to go for a walk, I know that's code for "Wanna talk?" And I love it. But how odd would it be if we went for a walk and stayed a good distance apart, not allowing us to really engage with each other? I wonder if we do this with God. I wonder if we say we "walk with God," but we keep at a distance that prevents closeness and communication.

"Walking *with* God" signifies a reciprocal relationship. It means communication and engagement from both God and us. God went first by initiating restored relationship through Jesus. He demonstrated His desire to walk in an ever-deepening relationship with us. What do we desire? As in any relationship that has depth and deep connection, there must be mutual pursuit. Intentional investment into an intimate relationship. Are we responding or resisting?

We can't expect to sense His withness without walking "with" Him. Consider Paul's words to the Colossians:

> And now, just as you accepted Christ Jesus as your Lord, you must continue to follow him. Let your roots grow down into him, and let your

> lives be built on him. Then your faith will grow strong in the truth you were taught, and you will overflow with thankfulness.
>
> Colossians 2:6–7 NLT

Could it be that a lot of us receive Jesus but then resist walking intimately with Him? We treat Him more like an insurance policy for eternity. We are tight-fisted with "our truth" rather than building our lives on The Truth. We don't grow deep roots in Him, and then we wonder why we aren't flourishing in our faith. We wonder why we don't overflow with thankfulness for His sacrifice or feel compelled to respond to His grace with obedience.

There is something in walking closely with Jesus that isn't experienced at a distance.

The irony is, the more willing we are to walk closely with Him, putting Him at the center of our life, or above all else we prioritize or pursue, the more we will experience the life we long for. He won't force himself on us. But oh, He'll pursue us! And He won't give up when we ignore Him. He is long-suffering. He is relentless with His love, but He will not coerce us to reciprocate. Honestly, sometimes I wish He would. And I especially wish this were true in the lives of people I love. Few things break my heart more than seeing loved ones ignoring or rejecting the love of God, and forfeiting the peace and purpose that comes in Him alone.

But He gives us free will because love that's fake or forced isn't love at all. He wants our love for Him to be the response of a heart that's been wrecked by His love for us. He has done every imaginable thing to make this possible. The rest lies in our response. I beg us not to resist His love.

God is not complicated, and He doesn't make relationship with us complicated. Oh yes, God's power and glory are beyond our comprehension, and His creation is wonderfully complex. But relationship with Him? Clear as can be!

God says,

> "You will seek me and find me, when you seek me with all your heart."
>
> Jeremiah 29:13

It's kinda that simple.

This verse is taken from a popular, and oft misapplied, passage that we'd benefit from reading together.

Chapter 29 is Jeremiah's letter to the exiles in Babylon, encouraging them to ignore the false teachers and advising them to carry on with their lives until God fulfills His promise to return them to Jerusalem.

Jeremiah writes in verses 11–14 (NIV):

> "For I know the plans I have for you," declares the LORD, "plans to prosper you and not to harm you, plans to give you hope and a future. Then you will call on me and come and pray to me, and I will listen to you. You will seek me and find me when you seek me with all your heart. I will be found by you," declares the LORD, "and will bring you back from captivity. I will gather you from all the nations and places where I have banished you," declares the LORD, "and will bring you back to the place from which I carried you into exile."

This passage is often presented with an accompanying message that says, "God wants to *improve* your life." It's not that He doesn't, but it's bigger than that. It would be better presented as, "God wants to *be* your life." We cannot claim this verse as a promise for prosperity in our present circumstances, but we can absolutely see it as confirmation of God's faithfulness to His people throughout all generations. We can read it as not "to us" but "for us."

Jeremiah was writing to a specific people for a specific time, but this passage is evidence of God's unchanging character and desire to be in personal relationship with His people.

This passage, as my friend Joel Muddamalle explains, holds "immense 'principle' for us today. While you and I are not under Babylonian imprisonment we are facing the impact and consequence of sin in our world. Today, we long for rescue and the final return of the King; Jesus. In a sense, things are much better for us because the fulfillment of God's promise to the Israelites was fulfilled on the cross. . . . Our 'prosperity' or good fortune is found in the salvation we received in Jesus."[1]

What God said to the exiles through Jeremiah is consistent with what God says to us today through Scripture. If we call on Him, He will listen to us. We will find Him when we seek Him "with all our heart."

But wait, this feels undoable. Right? Because deep down, we know we are people with divided hearts. Let me personalize that. I do not seek Him with my whole heart all the time. I ask Him to give me an undivided heart, but I feel the division daily! *Wholeheartedly* feels like a high bar! What are we to do when we flop? Ahh, yes. Fall on grace! He knows our hearts are fickle. He knows we get distracted by desires that don't take us deeper into His love. And still, what a miracle that He wants to be found by us. I promised you this wouldn't be about pursuing perfection, and it's not. It's about pursuing Him as He has pursued us so we can enjoy His presence and be changed by it!

This call to seek Him wholeheartedly reminds me that our God is a jealous God. But His jealousy is entirely unlike ours. Our jealousy is often described as a feeling of envy or suspicion toward relationships or possessions. It's often driven by poor self-image or low self-esteem. Need I say more about how and why God's jealousy is entirely unlike ours?

When God gives the Ten Commandments through Moses, we see God referring to himself as a jealous God in the second commandment.

> "You must not make for yourself an idol of any kind, or an image of anything in the heavens or on the earth or in the sea. You must not bow down to them or worship them, for I, the Lord your God, am a jealous God who will not tolerate your affection for any other gods."
>
> Deuteronomy 5:8–9

He wants our wholehearted attention and adoration, our complete devotion and worship because A, it belongs to Him and He is worthy of it, and B, our worship of anything else will deeply disappoint us, and that's at best. He is a wildly good God. He knows that intimacy with Him will bring us more pleasure and more satisfaction than anything else we're searching for. He knows that nothing and nobody compares to being found in Him. He knows that in "walking with Him" we get to experience what our soul wants most. Intimacy with Him. The enjoyment of His withness.

WORD

This kind of intimacy is what Paul describes in our key passage when he writes, "For His sake I have suffered the loss of all things and count them as rubbish, in order that I may gain Christ and be found in Him." Open your Bible, or return to page 7, and reread Philippians 3:8–11. Consider writing this passage on a piece of paper or sticky note and putting it where you will see it often. Rehearse it and commit it to memory.

SPIRIT

What do you sense the Holy Spirit stirring in you from your reading today? Journal your thoughts below about how you resist or respond to the invitation to seek Him wholeheartedly and enjoy intimacy.

DAY 10

How Do I Know I Am Growing in Intimacy with God?

When I became pregnant with our first son, Mike and I were living on the Upper West Side in New York City, which means we had countless dining options within blocks of us. But that didn't really matter because all I craved was Cap'n Crunch cereal and cheeseburgers. Oh, and Breyers mint chocolate chip ice cream. I know, so gross.

I remember one particular evening when I was having the worst nausea, and the only thing I could fathom eating was a Burger King cheeseburger. Pregnancy gave me the craziest cravings. Fortunately for Mike, there was a BK around the corner, so he ran down the stairs of our apartment building and then down Broadway for my burger. But the line was so long that by the time he got home, I almost gagged at the smell and told him the only thing I could fathom eating was now a McDonald's burger. No more BK for me.

Mike is a very good and patient man, and he once again ran down the stairs and up the block (taking the BK burger with him so the smell wouldn't kill me) and he came home shortly after with the meal of my dreams. Except that by then, all I could stomach was Cap'n Crunch, so I poured myself a bowl and cried over nothing. And Mike ate the McDonald's.

Changing cravings are common for us capricious humans. You don't have to be pregnant and hormonally unstable to have them. We all crave, all the time. And once we discover that the thing we were craving didn't truly satisfy the hunger in our soul, at least not for long, we then try to satisfy that hunger with the next thing, or just more of the same thing, until we finally come to the point where we must confess that there is only one thing that truly satisfies us. His name is Jesus. He does more than save us (though this would be enough). He satisfies us.

Think about it. Has there been a time in your life when you thought, *Finally, I have everything I want.* Even in prosperous seasons we still have that little voice that says, *Oh, but if I only had that one other little thing.* We are bottomless wells of desire. Desire that is intended to drive us to God!

God has "set eternity in the human heart," Ecclesiastes 3:11 (NIV). This teaches us that in every human heart is a God-given knowing that there is something more. And our hope comes from knowing that only in eternity, in our home with God, will we find the *complete* fulfillment we crave. Until then, we are invited to walk closely with God, getting glimpses of His glory, tasting His goodness, and satisfying our souls with the sweetness of His presence.

When we go to God to satisfy the growl in our soul, we know it means we are growing in intimacy with Him. What does this look like? Opening our Bibles. Sitting with Him in silence and solitude. Singing worship to Him, and speaking with Him throughout our day. It looks like seeking Him every time a worry needs to be reshaped into a prayer, setting our affection on Him again when we resurrect false idols, and seeing our sin as a personal offense against our holy and faithful God. It looks like staying in step with the Holy Spirit and going where He guides us rather than side-stepping Him into self-centered living. It looks like showing Satan the door when he breaks in as the thief who comes to steal our peace, kill our joy, and destroy our lives.

We know we're growing in intimacy when there is a sense of lostness when He isn't at the helm. It's missing Him when He feels far away (and it's never because He moved. We are the ones who scooch).

Finally, we know we are growing in intimacy when there is joy. Supernatural joy is a hallmark of a person who walks intimately with Jesus because joy is the fruit of the Spirit's presence. Christian joy, John Piper explains, "is a good feeling in the soul, produced by the Holy Spirit, as he causes us to see the beauty of Christ in the word and in the world."[1]

I love this description of joy. It's a good feeling *in the soul* that can only be produced by the Spirit. This joy is not caused by our circumstances but by seeing the beauty of Jesus. The beauty of Jesus never fades, and neither will our joy, *when* we are living intimately with Him. When I lack joy, I know it's a signal that my sight is set on all the things I can't fix or control, or on all the things I need to do. Joy *does* return when I choose to set my gaze on Jesus and allow Him to assure me of His presence in me.

Our souls long to adore *Him*. Our hearts ache to praise *Him*. And our resistance to this is not to our benefit! We are designed by God to desire deep intimacy with Him. Our souls are not unlike David's who, while fleeing his enemies in the wilderness, wrote:

> O God, you are my God; earnestly I seek you;
> my soul thirsts for you;
> my flesh faints for you,
> as in a dry and weary land where there is no water.
> So I have looked upon you in the sanctuary,
> beholding your power and glory.
> Because your steadfast love is better than life,
> my lips will praise you.
> So I will bless you as long as I live;
> in your name I will lift up my hands.
>
> My soul will be satisfied as with fat and rich food,
> and my mouth will praise you with joyful lips,
> when I remember you upon my bed,
> and meditate on you in the watches of the night;
> for you have been my help,
> and in the shadow of your wings I will sing for joy.
> My soul clings to you;
> your right hand upholds me.
>
> Psalm 63:1–8

Have you known this kind of longing for God? You don't have to be fleeing enemies to know this desperation for more of God. This is the kind of prayer one prays when one has tasted His goodness and is hungry for a touch of heaven again. Because life can be hard, and days can be long. Disappointments of daily life, an unexpected diagnosis, difficult relationships, dwindling bank accounts, dashed dreams, and more can steal our joy. These things are real and painful, and God doesn't ask us to overlook them. But He does invite us to find Him in them, and to reorient our hearts to satisfaction in Him while He works on our behalf.

"Your steadfast love is better than life" becomes our sincere heart's cry *when* we earnestly seek Him and set our affection on Him. But we can't do this on our own. We can't love God without the help of God. Our sin nature fights against putting God first. Our sin nature is stubborn. Living intimately with God, which is our greatest need, requires the Spirit of God. Because the Spirit of God cultivates intimacy.

The fundamental role of the Spirit is to make the love of Christ more than intellectual. He makes it experiential. Where there is merely information *about* God, He brings intimacy *with* God.

On Day 3, we studied Ephesians 3, where Paul prays that Christ may dwell in our hearts through faith. What I didn't mention then is that the Greek word translated "dwell" in verse 17 means to make himself at home. Paul is reminding us that only Christ, making himself at home in us, through His Spirit, will satisfy us. His presence will settle us. I want a settled soul. I'm thinking you do too! One that isn't anxious or often feeling empty. One that isn't constantly searching for something to stop the ache. The answer for a settled soul is intimacy with Jesus. A settled soul is one more indicator that we are growing in intimacy with God.

Our soul will reject substitutions. Counterfeit solutions will not fit the God-shaped soul with which we're born. I'm grateful He doesn't allow lesser things to fit. I want to be unsatisfied with anything less than Jesus.

Zephaniah 3:17 says, "The LORD your God is in your midst, a mighty one who will save; he will rejoice over you with gladness; he will quiet you by his love; he will exult over you with loud singing." This passage does more than tell us about the joy God had over His people in the

Old Testament. We find the fulfillment of this verse today in the Holy Spirit's presence among us. God is in our midst by His Spirit, He delights to dwell in us, He rejoices over us, and He satisfies us with His love.

WORD

Read what Paul wrote in 1 Thessalonians 1:1–10. Pay particular attention to verse 6 and what Paul teaches on joy given by the Holy Spirit. Journal your observations.

SPIRIT

As you read about some of the good indicators that we are growing in intimacy with God, what was the Spirit stirring in you? Pray and invite the Holy Spirit to yield an abundance of joy in your life that is rooted in intimacy with Jesus.

What Does Intimacy with God Produce in Us?

I spent most of my twenties trying to get God to like me. I knew He loved me (mostly because he "had to," ya know, since I put my trust in Jesus), but I wasn't so sure he liked me. Why did I feel like this? Mostly because I was putting my hope in my effort to live rightly, which wasn't perfectly. So I assumed He was regularly disappointed in me. I had yet to comprehend that God doesn't like me based on my ability to live like Christ, and that no amount of obedience makes me righteous. You can imagine the freedom that quite literally washed over me when I was enabled by the Spirit to see in the Word how everything I was trying to include on my résumé of "righteousness" was "as rubbish." I can't exaggerate the difference it made in my life with Christ to believe that righteousness comes by faith alone, in Christ alone.

This is the life-altering difference Paul writes about in our key passage, so let's read it together again.

> Indeed, I count everything as loss because of the surpassing worth of knowing Christ Jesus my Lord. For his sake I have suffered the loss of all things and count them as rubbish, in order that I may gain Christ and be found in him, not having a righteousness of my own that comes from the law, but that which comes through faith in Christ, the righteousness from God that depends on faith—that I may know him and the power of his

> resurrection, and may share his sufferings, becoming like him in his death, that by any means possible I may attain the resurrection from the dead.
>
> Philippians 3:8–11

Knowing Christ is more than collecting facts about Christ. The knowing Paul is talking about isn't superficial or surface level. It's the kind of knowing and being known that transforms our lives from the inside out.

When Paul says that his accomplishments are "as rubbish" compared with being *found in Him*, he means that he values oneness with Christ above all else! He treasures being irrevocably united with Christ and covered in the righteousness of Christ.

When Paul writes to "know him and the power of his resurrection," he knows that God's presence and power are coursing through him. Ultimately, he is certain he will experience this resurrection power from the dead, even as he will share in Christ's sufferings before he will share in His resurrection!

Can we, like Paul, say that we consider our achievements "as rubbish" compared with knowing Christ? It's one thing for me to *say* it, but it's another thing for me to *live* it. This is something I have to often, and honestly, assess in my own life, because the human tendency is to return to our résumé.

How does prizing Christ become more than lip service? Through intimacy *with* Christ!

When there is holy intimacy, there is assurance of identity. Lesser things lose their power to define us when we have a deep life with God. Obedience isn't what we rely on to justify ourselves when we are in intimate relationship with God. This doesn't mean we lose our drive for kingdom-building living. This doesn't mean we become careless with the unique purpose placed on our life. It means these things no longer define us or determine our worth. They are the things we do *because* we are found in Christ, for the glory of Christ. This is the faithfulness and freedom that I prayed, and continue to pray, we will experience through these pages together.

Paul goes on to say,

> Not that I have already obtained this or am already perfect, but I press on to make it my own, because Christ Jesus has made me his own. Brothers, I do not consider that I have made it my own. But one thing I do: forgetting what lies behind and straining forward to what lies ahead, I press on toward the goal for the prize of the upward call of God in Christ Jesus.
>
> Philippians 3:12–14

"Christ Jesus has made me His own!" Are there more beautiful words we could ever utter? Say with me, "I am chosen by Christ!"

This makes me think about what happens on the playground when two kids select themselves as captains and then take turns choosing people for their team. There are few things that feel worse for a child than watching others get selected while they stand there, holding their breath, hoping to be the next one whose name is called. *Choose me!* their insides scream, while they try to play it cool.

But with Jesus, you never need to hold your breath, hoping to be chosen. You're not waiting for your name to be called. You were chosen on the cross over 2,000 years ago. Christ has made you His own and freely offered you a place on His team. A place in eternity with Him! A life of purpose today! Not because of anything you bring but because of what His blood accomplished.

From (not for!) this position of security and acceptance, we press ahead for the prize of heavenly citizenship. The goal is to know Him and the power of His resurrection.

It's been said that the gospel isn't opposed to effort, it's opposed to earning. I'm actually going to repeat myself because it's *that* important. The gospel isn't opposed to effort. It's opposed to earning. This is precisely what Paul is talking about.

Something else worth noting about this passage is that Paul is alluding to a race. But in this race, the outcome isn't dependent on our physical strength or our spiritual grit. Christ has supplied the supernatural strength. He has given us the Spirit to propel us until we reach the prize. But we still need to participate.

Effort is required of us if we want to go deeper with God and enjoy a vibrant relationship with Him. We, like Paul, have to make knowing Him the goal. But when we show up, Jesus supplies the power of the Holy Spirit—in abundance.

Jesus emptied himself of power on the cross so we could be filled with it! He provides the power to run toward Him, toward heaven, where we will enjoy uninterrupted fellowship with God.

If you're not compelled to invest the time and make the sacrifice, ask the Holy Spirit to magnify the incomparable beauty of Jesus to your heart. Ask the Holy Spirit to also show you the ugliness of your sin compared with the beauty of God, because "the living water of grace is sweet only to those who know the bitter taste of their sin."[1] We can't authentically declare the words to John Newton's hymn, "Amazing grace! how sweet the sound, That saved a wretch like me" without letting the Holy Spirit put a magnifying glass over our deficiency. We don't do this to lead us to despair. We do this to lead us to desperation for and delight in God. Because there is only absolution, not condemnation, in Christ!

I'm not ashamed to confess the wretchedness of my sin because I have been given a new identity in Christ. An identity not based on what I have done or what's been done to me. An identity not based on what others see in me or say about me. An identity not based on anything I have accomplished or earned. It's an identity rooted in the righteousness Christ bestowed on me.

Paul explains it this way:

> Therefore, if anyone is in Christ, he is a new creation. The old has passed away; behold, the new has come. All this is from God, who through Christ reconciled us to himself. . . . For our sake he made him to be sin who knew no sin, so that in him we might become the righteousness of God.
>
> 2 Corinthians 5:17–18, 21

When you are found in Christ, you are a new creation. God didn't reconcile us to himself to make us better but to make us blameless! Brand new. This is all God's doing, through His son.

I am who Jesus says I am. You are who Jesus says you are. We are empowered to live out our God-given identity through God-initiated intimacy with the same confidence that inhabited Paul.

WORD

Read 2 Corinthians 5:11–21 for more context on the passage we just read. Pay special attention to verses 14–15, again stressing how it is His love that compels us to no longer live for ourselves. Journal your thoughts.

SPIRIT

What do you sense the Holy Spirit is stirring in you or saying to you from your reading today? Pray that the Holy Spirit would free you from trying to earn God's love through right living, and empower you to press on because Christ's righteousness is yours by faith alone.

DAY 12

What Inhibits Intimacy with God?

We know from our relationships with one another that intimacy requires vulnerability. If you were to call to mind a few of your relationships that are characterized by deep connection and affection, whether with a friend, spouse, or sibling, I'm guessing those relationships are ones in which you feel safe to let down your guard and allow them to see the real you. The you with insecurities and scars and maybe even open wounds. As I do this exercise myself, and think about the relationships in my life that are the deepest and dearest to me, I see vulnerability woven into the fabric of each.

Vulnerability is courageous. It's tender. It's essential to connection. And it requires trust. But trusting can be scary. I can't imagine there is a single one of us who hasn't been hurt or let down after being willing to be vulnerable and trust someone with our fragile heart.

Of course, not everyone deserves our vulnerability. We must choose wisely. And even when we choose wisely, we will get hurt because we are all flawed human beings. Even those of us who genuinely desire to live lives that reflect the holiness of God will mess up, and often. When trust is broken, we have to do the good work of rebuilding because, as I tell my sons, "Without trust, we don't have much." This doesn't mean grace doesn't exist in the relationship. It does, in abundance. In fact, grace is the very thing meant to lead us to repentance and repair of the relationship.

As it is in our human relationships, vulnerability (and therefore trust) is at the heart of intimacy with God. The difference with God is that He has never broken trust with us. We are the untrustworthy party. We broke trust with Him. Yet we can be so skeptical of Him. Why do we doubt His goodness and question His motives when He has been nothing but faithful from generation to generation?

Because He will never fail us, we can—with confidence—echo the psalmist who declared,

> For the LORD is good; his steadfast love endures forever, and his faithfulness to all generations.
>
> Psalm 100:5

He is altogether good! His love is perfect; it perseveres and prevails! He is completely faithful and trustworthy. We are safe in His love.

And because He is incapable of letting us down, we can—with confidence—echo the prophet Jeremiah, who declared:

> The steadfast love of the LORD never ceases;
> his mercies never come to an end;
> they are new every morning;
> great is your faithfulness.
>
> Lamentations 3:22–23

His mercy can't stop. His mercy won't stop. Every sunrise greets us with steadfast love and fresh mercy. But there's something else in this passage that I only recently learned. The word *mercy* can also be translated as *compassion*. This hit me differently. I awake to the compassion of God. You awake to the compassion of God. A harsh day may await us, but we are carried by His compassion for us. This is more than mercy. See, mercy is God not giving us what we deserve for our mess-ups. We deserve eternal judgement. But because He is merciful, we don't get what we deserve. But His compassion goes even further. It offers another and another and another welcome to restoration.

This is what His faithfulness looks like. He can be trusted wholeheartedly with our hearts.

But maybe trusting God feels risky to you. Maybe you've experienced enough pain and disappointment that you wonder if He *really* is good and His love *really* is perfect and your heart *really* is safe with Him. You're not sure this is a "risk" you are willing to take.

Friend, if this is you, can I encourage you? If we will commit to pursuing Him and prizing Him, and trusting Him with our whole hearts, we *will* see and experience His goodness.

Paul reassures us,

> No one who trusts God like this—heart and soul—will ever regret it.
>
> Romans 10:11 MESSAGE

Think about it this way: Is there anyone you can count on to *never* let you down? A parent? A spouse? A best friend? Me neither. As hard as we try to be loyal and loving to those we care deeply about, we say and do things we wish we could take back. We hurt each other. People will disappoint us. A world riddled with sin will disappoint us. Life may not look like we think it should. Miracles may not come when we expect them to. But God does not lie to us. He is a promise keeper. And He is for our good.

So even though we are good at blaming God for our pain and undesirable outcomes, it is never God who disappoints. That's the devil's job. He is full of empty promises and shaming narratives. And he is so good at disguising himself that we point our finger at God. Our enemy doesn't come with horns and a tail, telling us all about his goal to destroy us and ensure that we don't have intimacy with the Lover of our soul. Satan "masquerades as an angel of light" (2 Corinthians 11:14 NIV), presenting evil in a good light, leading us deeper into discontentment and doubt of God's grace so we can't bear to bring our messy, unholy selves before a holy God because we have listened to the lies that tell us we are the exception to God's grace.

See, struggling to trust God with our heart isn't the only barrier to intimacy. Sometimes we struggle to trust that God truly welcomes the real us. The one we don't want anyone else knowing about. What if we risk taking Him all of our brokenness, only to be told we're hopeless? I don't mean to simplify this, but the truth is that nobody has ever come to Jesus whole. We all come broken and helpless. But never hopeless. And never rejected.

Running into His arms is the very thing that will revive you. In His arms, the authenticity of His love is affirmed, the fear of "too broken" is dispelled, and the transforming power of His grace is experienced. We don't leave the same.

Are there other barriers to intimacy? There are, and the writer of Hebrews explains this well:

> Don't be obsessed with getting more material things. Be relaxed with what you have. Since God assured us, "I'll never let you down, never walk off and leave you," we can boldly quote,
>
> God is there, ready to help;
> I'm fearless no matter what.
> Who or what can get to me?
>
> Hebrews 13:5–6 Message

This teaching was given in regard to greed and our insatiable desire for more. It shows us that greed also gets in the way of intimacy. We are tempted to not trust His provision. We fear our God of abundance is actually a God of scarcity. We elevate what we want Him to give us or do for us above who He is for us.

Sometimes we think we are living in an intimate relationship with God when it's really more of a transactional one. The thing that takes my breath away is how He is so tolerant when we treat Him like a transactional God.

Our priority is clarity. His is closeness.

Our priority is instructions. His is intimacy.

Our priority is formulas. His is friendship.

Does this resonate with you? I go to God asking for clarity on a decision my husband and I are making. But God says, "Come closer." I go to God wanting instructions and next steps for a dream I'm chasing, but God says, "Spend time with me." I go to God wanting a formula for overcoming a temptation that keeps stalking me, but God says, "Daughter, lean on me." This isn't to suggest He won't provide clarity, wisdom, or power. He has promised these benefits to us. But these benefits are the overflow of a deeply personal relationship with Him. He will answer on His terms, in His perfect timing. He gets to do that because He is God and He alone knows what is for our good and His glory.

He is after closeness and deep friendship because that is the birthplace of faithfulness, growth, and power. Relationship with Him produces these invaluable things in our lives.

Will you put your full weight on His "precious and very great promises" (2 Peter 1:4)? And I mean your *full* weight. Not like when I step on the scale after a season of indulging and try to not put my full weight on the scale for fear it will confirm what my zipper has spoken. Not that kind of weight. Your all.

Intimacy with Jesus brings incomparable peace and joy. May our hearts be so swept up in His love that the barriers we've built, or the lies we've believed, be washed away in the safety of His presence.

WORD

Read Romans 8:38–39. Nothing can separate us from God's love! He can be trusted with our hearts. We are safe in His embrace.

SPIRIT

Invite the Holy Spirit to bring to mind the barriers to intimacy with Jesus in your life. Journal those things below, and invite the Holy Spirit to help you surrender those things and trust His "precious and very great promises."

DAY 13

Does God Really Want to Be Found by Me?

Our seven-year-old son, Finn, loves to play hide-and-seek. And he's gotten quite creative at hiding. It can be real work to find him. In fact, on some days I haven't been able to find him. I've just declared "You win" at the top of my lungs, hoping he'll reappear with pride on his face for the epic hiding spot he can return to when we play again.

I remember when our three older boys were around Finn's age and I was the one who wanted to play hide-and-seek just so I could get a few minutes alone. I *really* hid! I didn't just plop down behind a couch so they'd find me quickly. The sheer exhaustion that can be part of parenting multiple little ones can motivate you to seek respite wherever you can. Even if that's in a game of hide-and-seek.

Sometimes I wonder if we think life with God is a bit like a game of hide-and-seek. When we are the seekers, we wonder, "Does He *really* want to be found by me?" And when we hide from Him, does He really come seeking us like the one sheep who was lost out of the one hundred?[a] Or does He enjoy the break because we can be *a lot*?

Do you ever wonder, *Does He really desire deep friendship with me? I can be so disappointing. And difficult. I'm afraid I just let Him down all the time. I don't even know if I know how to be friends with God.*

a. Matthew 18:10–14 reference.

James is helpful here. Let's read what he has to say.

> You adulterous people! Do you not know that friendship with the world is enmity with God? Therefore whoever wishes to be a friend of the world makes himself an enemy of God. Or do you suppose it is to no purpose that the Scripture says, "He yearns jealously over the spirit that he has made to dwell in us"? But he gives more grace. Therefore it says, "God opposes the proud but gives grace to the humble." Submit yourselves therefore to God. Resist the devil, and he will flee from you. Draw near to God, and he will draw near to you.
>
> James 4:4–8

There is a lot of good stuff to unpack in this passage. First, there is a choice to make: friendship with the world, embracing the ways of the world, or friendship with God, by imitating Christ.

God desires closeness with us so much that the Holy Spirit in us yearns jealously over us. But don't misunderstand this jealousy. It's unlike ours. His jealousy demonstrates His commitment to seeing His joy made complete in us. This is holy jealousy. God the Spirit is motivated by passionate devotion to our good and God's glory in our lives. Whatever threatens to steal our affection for our Savior stirs Him to protectiveness. I have to say, I find this holy jealousy heartening, wholly unlike human jealousy that feels threatening.

Yet even when we are lured by the ways of the world, He gives "more grace." He knows we will hurt the Holy Spirit with our sin, but His grace inspires us to come "home" again and again. Not only that, but His Spirit in us keeps helping us resist the distractions and temptations of life in a fallen world.

Jesus modeled perfectly how to be involved in the world without imitating the way of the world. He didn't hide out as He lived His human life. He engaged fully but never let the priorities of a fallen and sinful world dictate His lifestyle. He wasn't changed by people as He engaged with them. He was the difference maker. And by His Spirit within us, the same can be true of us. Maybe you've heard the expression that "we are called to be *in* the world but not *of* the world." This is what James is teaching. He isn't instructing us to remove ourselves *from* culture but rather to live in God's transforming love and power *in* culture. To shine light into darkness (while also knowing our limits and what tempts us—we must be wise).

Imitating Christ requires drawing near *to* Him and drawing *on* Him so His power is manifested in your life to resist the devil.

So when James writes "Draw near to God, and He will draw near to you," he isn't suggesting that God is nervous but will feel safe to respond if you go first. God already went first in Jesus!

We often see "Draw near to God, and He will draw near to you" as an inspirational meme or on a lovely wooden sign placed on a bookshelf. The wording makes us feel welcome. But it doesn't end there, and we can't ignore what James writes immediately following it. The next few sentences might not look as cute on a wooden sign on our shelf:

> Cleanse your hands, you sinners, and purify your hearts, you double-minded. Be wretched and mourn and weep. Let your laughter be turned to mourning and your joy to gloom. Humble yourselves before the Lord, and he will exalt you.
>
> James 4:9–10

In the Old Testament, before the priests could come to God in the tabernacle, they had to wash their hands and feet in the basin as a symbol of spiritual purification. Hence the instruction in this passage to "cleanse your hands" and "purify your hearts." What are we to do about this today?

Let's start with the good news. Jesus made a way for us to draw near to God, even when we feel filthy and guilty. Jesus is our purification. Even as active sinners who are "double-minded" we can boldly draw near to God because we are cleansed by the blood of Jesus!

If there is bad news, I guess it would be that we must humble ourselves. I call this the bad news because humbling ourselves is hard. Confessing that we need to have our hands cleansed and our hearts purified doesn't come easily. We want to be able to tell Him how hard we've been working and how well we've been doing. But instead, we are told to mourn and weep over our sin, which is not merely breaking the rules but breaking God's heart. A right view of our sin *should* turn our laughter to mourning. Nothing funny about what our sin caused our Savior.

James is describing what it looks like to come to the Lord with a sincerely repentant heart. This is, I believe, the heartbeat of intimacy with God. Confession and repentance.

"Confession is the way we trust the grace we say we believe in. It's the way we acknowledge that God doesn't love us because we *are* lovely; his love *makes* us lovely. And it equips us to love."[1]

Confession and repentance are where our gloom returns to joy! We are fully forgiven and lavishly loved!

Will we humble ourselves? Will we acknowledge the ways we fall short each day and thank Jesus for being our sinless sacrifice who gives us His perfect record and calls us His precious child? Will we declare His greatness as David did in Psalm 145?

> The LORD is righteous in all his ways
> and kind in all his works.
> The LORD is near to all who call on him,
> to all who call on him in truth.
> He fulfills the desire of those who fear him;
> he also hears their cry and saves them.
> The LORD preserves all who love him,
> but all the wicked he will destroy.
>
> My mouth will speak the praise of the Lord
> and let all flesh bless his holy name forever and ever.
>
> Psalm 145:17–21

The Lord is righteous *and* kind. He is near to all who call on Him *in truth*, which means with godly integrity. When we live in healthy fear of Him (meaning that we have a right view of His holiness, justice, and authority that leads us to live in awe and respect and honor of Him), He not only hears our cries but saves us.

This is the last of the Psalms of David, a godly king who knows his God intimately and knows the power of His forgiveness and redemption when he repents, and it compels him to awe and adoration.

Like David, we must humble ourselves and acknowledge how we have sinned against our holy God. He calls us to grieve over our sin and submit to His lordship.

He isn't hiding from you. He wants to be found by you. He welcomes you with wide-open arms as His cleansed and cherished child!

WORD

Open your Bible and read all of Psalm 145. Pay special attention to verses 8–9. How does this affirm or disrupt your beliefs about God's character and His welcome of you? Journal your thoughts below.

SPIRIT

What is the Holy Spirit stirring in you? Pray and draw near to God. Confess your sins and be still in His loving presence. Let His love and forgiveness wash over you!

DAY 14

What Is Repentance?

I'm curious about what images come to mind when you hear the word *repent.*

Maybe the image is an angry dude with a sign about hell, yelling on a street corner? Or a preacher behind a pulpit with a stern look on his face and a message of judgement on his tongue? Or maybe it's something softer, such as a woman on her knees with remorse in her heart, or a teenager talking to God through a tear-drenched pillow.

I'd also like you to think about the emotions or words you associate with repentance. Crushing guilt? Or shame that stings? Accusation or anger? Or are they something more like relief, refreshment, a fresh start?

I ask these questions because I think repentance has gotten a bad rap due to the way some folks have misused it to instill unhealthy fear about our eternal future, or to keep us in line until we get there. But I believe Jesus had a different posture than the people we see on some corners or behind certain pulpits when He preached on repentance. And I'm hopeful we will see repentance for the gift it is as we learn more about it. So we are going to camp out on repentance for several days, because this practice is critical to moving into a deeper life with Jesus. Without it, we stay in the shallows.

Let's turn to Matthew 4, where we see Jesus begin to preach after He defeated the devil's tempting in the wilderness.

> Now when he heard that John had been arrested, he withdrew into Galilee. And leaving Nazareth he went and lived in Capernaum by the sea. . . .

> From that time Jesus began to preach, saying, "Repent, for the kingdom of heaven is at hand."
>
> Matthew 4:12–13, 17

"From that time" indicates a crucial turning point in the life of Jesus. He is beginning His public ministry, and His message cannot be clearer: "Repent! Because the reign of God that He brings about through Me, His Son, is coming!"

The Greek word for repentance is *metanoia*, coming from *meta* (which means to change) and *noein* (a mental perspective). It means to have a change of mind or heart that leads to a change in direction. Repentance is a deliberate turning from sin to holiness, rebellious living to righteous living, obstinance to obedience.

There are generally two approaches to repentance. The first is an attitude of attrition, which is more about fear of punishment or concern over losing something or someone valuable to you due to your decision or action. The second is contrition, and I don't think it comes as any surprise that this is the heart posture God desires. Contrition causes a believer to sorrow because they recognize that their sin is what nailed their Savior to the cross. Contrition occurs when we acknowledge that our sin, first and foremost, has offended our holy God. Contrite people grieve their sin because they hold their sin up to God's holiness and Christ's sacrifice.

So repentance is more than a casual "I'm sorry, God." It's more than feeling regretful. Repentance is a daily practice of acknowledging that we have sinned against a holy God. It's sorrow for wrongdoing that leads to a change of heart and mind. It's sincerely saying, "Lord, change my mind about my sin. Help me see my sin the way you do!"

The complication here is that we don't always feel sorrow. Sometimes we don't even feel sorry. We fall into the attrition category. We might even *like* our sin or minimize it while we "repent" to try to avoid consequences; but we have no real intention or plan not to return to that sin again. Sometimes, maybe we doubt we have the power to turn from it, so we succumb to it.

The late Tim Keller wrote, "True repentance begins where whitewashing ('Nothing really happened') and blame shifting ('It wasn't really my fault') and self-pity ('I'm sorry because of what it has cost *me*') and self-flagellation ('I will feel so terrible no one will be able to criticize me') end."[1]

So if you aren't feeling sorrow over your sin (this helps me when I am hardhearted and self-righteous) ask the Holy Spirit to awaken your spirit to your whitewashing, blame shifting, self-pity, or self-flagellation. Ask Him to break your heart over the same things that break God's. Ask Him to tenderize your heart to the price Jesus paid on the cross. Ask Him to remind you who and where you'd be if it weren't for Jesus. Remember that judgement and punishment are what we deserve, but grace and forgiveness are what we receive. Because of Jesus.

This isn't about being ashamed of yourself over your sin. Jesus bore your shame on the cross when He bore your sin. Please don't miss that! Contrary to what the devil—our accuser—would have you believe, Jesus does not want you to punish yourself for something He already took the punishment for. Shame settled on Jesus so it could be lifted off you. You are clean! You are free!

So while this conversation is not about feeling ashamed, it *is* about having a right understanding of our utter lack of righteousness outside of Jesus, and acknowledging that repentance leads to the forgiveness that cleanses us.

This is also about being freed—completely—from the pain of carrying our sin and shame, and empowered to experience the fullness of His love and the warmth of His presence. The day I felt Jesus lift the coat of shame off me was one of the most powerful and precious days of my life. I wasn't attending a Christian women's conference or sitting on my counselor's couch (although these are often places where God does great work in our hearts!). I was in my home with my Bible open on my lap while my young kids napped. I went to Him desperate, and He delivered. Indeed His Word is alive and active! This was where my freedom started.

"All have sinned and fall short of the glory of God," as we read in Romans 3:23, is just one of many verses that remind us we *all* need

Jesus. Not only have we all sinned against Him and fallen short of His glory, but we never graduate from needing His grace. We might resist His grace, or avoid it as though we're allergic to it, but His grace is sufficient to keep covering our sin. It is enough!

I believe we are growing as Jesus followers when we are becoming more and more convinced of how short we fall at obeying God's law and how much we need His grace.

As our lives look more and more like Christ's through sanctification by the Spirit, I also hope our hearts will become more and more amazed that He continues to love us and be deeply committed to our good despite the fact that we will continue to do what we know we ought not do.

So when you find yourself asking, "How can I get free from this sin?" start with confession and repentance! Confession is to say what is true.[2] But we can't stop there if we want to be free from it. We need to confess it and turn from it. That is repentance. Repentance is a deliberate act because we won't accidentally turn from sin. We can't just hope it will happen. The enemy of our soul is far too committed to tempting us to turn away from God's best for us. Jesus' invitation to repentance requires a response. We must deliberately return to God. And by His grace, we can! And because of His grace, His forgiveness will always be found.

I love *The Message* paraphrase of Romans 8:1–4:

> Those who enter into Christ's being-here-for-us no longer have to live under a continuous, low-lying black cloud. A new power is in operation. The Spirit of life in Christ, like a strong wind, has magnificently cleared the air, freeing you from a fated lifetime of brutal tyranny at the hands of sin and death.
>
> God went for the jugular when he sent his own Son. He didn't deal with the problem as something remote and unimportant. In his Son, Jesus, he personally took on the human condition, entered the disordered mess of struggling humanity in order to set it right once and for all.

We will never be met with rejection in repentance. We won't receive a lecture on how badly we've dropped the ball—again. Only forgiveness and healing and refreshment of our souls. Oh, and power. We can't forget the power. We don't repent to go right back to sin. The Holy Spirit in us empowers us to pursue Christ and His righteousness!

WORD

Open your Bible and read all of 2 Peter chapter 3. Notice the assurance of God's faithfulness to finish what He started. Journal how this applies to you.

SPIRIT

What is the Holy Spirit stirring in you? Pray and allow the Holy Spirit to lead you in repentance. Receive the forgiveness and refreshment Christ gives.

DAY 15

Who Leads Us to Repentance?

The first thesis of Martin Luther's *Ninety-Five Theses* reads: "When our Lord and Master, Jesus Christ, said 'Repent,' He called for the entire life of believers to be one of repentance."[1]

At first this might sound like Luther is leading us to constantly rehearse all the ways we fall short. That would keep me pretty busy. Could that be right?

Well, yes and no. What Jesus wants is for you to be free! "For *freedom* Christ has set us free" (Galatians 5:1, emphasis added). But we are really good at running back to slavery. Slavery to sin. Slavery to shame. Slavery to striving for a righteousness that's already ours in Jesus. This is not a new phenomenon, by the way. The Israelites said they'd rather go back to slavery in Egypt than wait on God in the desert, in Exodus 16. We are quick to settle for familiarity over freedom.

But repentance helps us live freely!

Luther is teaching that repentance is not a one and done. It isn't something we only do to receive salvation through Christ. We are to do it again and again for sanctification through the Spirit, and it is the Holy Spirit who leads us there.

Our repentance originates from the Holy Spirit. Imagine Him taking your hand into His and saying, "Come with me to talk with Jesus. Let me lead you to freedom from all of this. Freedom from trying to save yourself by keeping God's commands. Freedom from always feeling like a failure. Freedom from being owned by your sin." Where the Spirit of the Lord leads, there is *freedom*![a]

Jesus clearly communicates how the Spirit plays this distinct role in the Trinity. Jesus teaches us that the Holy Spirit is the agent of salvation who reveals Jesus to us as the one Mediator and only hope for reconciling God and man. Without the Spirit, we would have zero awareness of the atrociousness of our sin and the splendor of our Savior. The Gospel of John records these words from Jesus about the Spirit:

> And when he comes, he will convict the world concerning sin and righteousness and judgment: concerning sin, because they do not believe in me; concerning righteousness, because I go to the Father, and you will see me no longer; concerning judgment, because the ruler of this world is judged.
>
> John 16:8–11

He convicts us concerning sin, meaning He convinces us we need Jesus because of our sin. He convicts us concerning righteousness, meaning He shows us how safe we are in the complete righteousness of Jesus that covers us. And finally, He convicts us concerning judgement, meaning He convinces us that Jesus holds the victory over Satan, and our enemy and death have no authority over us.

Do we know what a gift this is? For us to be convinced of our need to repent to receive salvation, the Holy Spirit must expose it and convict us of it.

Not long ago, Mike and I were out to dinner with a small group of friends when one of the men at the table mentioned the distance at which I was holding my menu. "Do you think it might be time for you to join the rest of us with our readers?" he joked. The truth is, I hadn't even thought of needing readers. Not once. My last eye exam confirmed I still had perfect vision. But just a few months later, I'd begun to hold things like menus, books, and my phone farther and farther away without even realizing what I was doing.

a. 2 Corinthians 3:17 reference.

The next day I purchased readers from a local boutique in town. If I was going to wear readers, they were going to be cute. Very cute.

I put those 1.0 glasses on and pulled out my phone to test them out. I gasped. I could not believe how much better I could see. The readers were a need I didn't even know I had.

What my friend did for me is a lot like what the Holy Spirit does for us. He gives us godly glasses, gives us spiritual sight. He gives us awareness of our need. Of our sin.

This sin-exposing ministry of the Spirit continues throughout our entire life *so that* we are conformed more and more into the image of the One we worship and love: Jesus (see Romans 8:29).

For example, when there is bad fruit in our lives, we need the Holy Spirit to help us taste how bitter our sin is. Is it loose lips that engage in unnecessary talk or language that doesn't edify the person we're talking to? Is it overindulgence in the things we enjoy? Is it choices that God clearly tells us to completely avoid? Is it a sour attitude about not getting what we want from God or an unforgiving or critical spirit with someone who hurt us? In all these places and many more, we need the Spirit's conviction so we will continue to be conformed into the likeness of the One we love and want our life to testify to!

Now, maybe you're asking, "Does it really matter that we know it's the work of the Holy Spirit in us? Why do I need to know He's the One who leads me to repentance? Isn't it enough that I know repentance is required for a deeper life with God?" Oh, friend, it matters greatly!

To enjoy an intimate relationship with God, we are going to need to be open to and cooperative with the Spirit. We'll need to trust Him and be trusting of what He's been given to do in our lives.

And our pursuit of sin (or our lack of repentance) grieves the Spirit of God in us. Paul explains it this way:

> And do not grieve the Holy Spirit of God, by whom you were sealed for the day of redemption. Let all bitterness and wrath and anger and clamor and slander be put away from you, along with all malice.
>
> Ephesians 4:30–31

The Greek word translated "grieve" in Ephesians 4:30 is *lupeó* and it can mean "to make sorrowful; to affect with sadness, cause grief; to throw into sorrow."[2]

God the Spirit grieves because our pursuit of sin is destructive in our lives. But also because of this: sin is never siloed. Our bitterness, rage, anger, harsh words, and slander does more than bring grief to our own souls. It has spillover effects onto others who are also made in His image. Most important, our sin interrupts our bond of affection and connection with Jesus, and it prevents us from walking freely in the costly freedom He purchased for us. Sin is oppressive, a weight we weren't meant to carry. Repentance and the receiving of forgiveness lifts the burden. It frees us. This is His "for us" love.

The Message paraphrase of Ephesians 4:30 helps us see this so clearly:

> Don't grieve God. Don't break his heart. His Holy Spirit, moving and breathing in you, is the most intimate part of your life, making you fit for himself. Don't take such a gift for granted.

I'm grateful Paul doesn't leave us in the don'ts. He does more than tell us what we shouldn't do because it grieves the Spirit of God. He tells us how to, shall we say, cheer the Spirit, how to draw closer to Jesus, and how to glorify God.

> Be kind to one another, tenderhearted, forgiving one another, as God in Christ forgave you.
>
> Ephesians 4:32

Emulating Jesus through our kindness, tenderheartedness, and forgiveness of one another is the way forward. A relational list from a relational God. It makes sense, doesn't it!

In closing today, because I know we can bring a lot of baggage into a conversation about repentance, I want to read what Peter, the apostle of Jesus, writes to us:

> The Lord is not slow to fulfill his promise as some count slowness, but is patient toward you, not wishing that any should perish, but that all should reach repentance.
>
> 2 Peter 3:9

He patiently waits for our repentance because He does not want us to perish! He wants us to be forever in fellowship with Him! If we can see repentance as more about giving Jesus His rightful place in our heart as the treasure of our life and not about beating ourselves up for not getting it right, we might just start to look forward to this daily practice.

WORD

Open your Bible and read Ephesians 4:17–32, where Paul writes about our new life in the Spirit. Journal anything the Spirit highlights for you as you read, and consider His invitation to you in what He highlights.

SPIRIT

Invite the Holy Spirit to show you where you are grieving Him, or causing Him sorrow. Thank Him for giving you godly glasses, and seek the Lord's healing and forgiveness. Receive the forgiveness and freedom with a grateful heart!

DAY 16

What Leads Us to Repentance?

I want us to think back on our childhoods and recall how our parents or caregivers tended to motivate us to confess our wrongdoing, to feel genuine sorrow when we messed up. How did they persuade us to own our mistakes and choose differently going forward?

I'm asking us to do this because we often assume that God interacts with us—as a Father—in a way similar to what we've experienced with our earthly father, mother, or caregiver. "There is interesting research that finds a correlation between your relationship with your parents, particularly your father, and your initial view of who God is and how much we want a relationship with Him," according to Pepperdine University.[1]

If our parents were empowered by the Spirit to reflect the Father's heart when they disciplined us, this would likely cause us to see God as One who leads with love. But even the best earthly fathers get it wrong, discipline imperfectly, and are incapable of perfect love. And if our parents did not reflect the heart of God when they disciplined us, it would likely cause us to see God as One who leads with fear, threats, and wrath.

When I say "God as One who leads with love," I'm not suggesting that God doesn't discipline His children. Love is not the absence of discipline. In fact, discipline is evidence of love; Scripture tells us not to "take the Lord's discipline lightly or lose heart when you are reproved by him, for the Lord disciplines the one he loves" (Hebrews 12:5–6 CSB).

God gives us guardrails within which to live. God calls us to obedience and holiness. God disciplines us "for our benefit, so that we can share in his holiness" (Hebrews 12:10 CSB). And God calls us to repentance when we don't share in His holiness. But here is what I don't want us to miss: God doesn't lead us back to His heart with fear, threats, and wrath. He leads us back with kindness.

Paul asks,

> Or do you presume on the riches of his kindness and forbearance and patience, not knowing that God's kindness is meant to lead you to repentance?
>
> Romans 2:4

Kindness, forbearance, and patience are not always a parent's first instinct in leading kids to have repentant hearts. Parenting this way requires a deep dependence on the Spirit and an experience of God's grace in your own life.

But God? His instinct is kindness.

God's wild kindness is meant to turn His kids (you and me!) to repentance. But how easy it is to "presume on" or take for granted the riches of His kindness, to dismiss the severity of our sin, and forgo the sweetness of forgiveness.

Oftentimes, when we refer to Paul's teaching on repentance, we only talk about the verse we just read. It's the teaching that's easier to digest. But because the Jews, at the time this was written, misunderstood God's patience with their sin as God's lack of judgement of sin, Paul needed to ensure they understood God's motive. So Paul goes on to say,

> But because of your hard and impenitent heart you are storing up wrath for yourself on the day of wrath when God's righteous judgment will be revealed.
>
> Romans 2:5

It's more fun to think on the kindness of God than to think on His wrath. But verse 5 is actually good news! The wrath we store up for ourselves with our sin has been satisfied in the sacrifice of His Son, Jesus.

Jesus absorbed the full fury of God, for the rebellion that created a great chasm between us and His holiness.

If you're a parent, let me ask you this: How badly does your heart break over the choices your kids make that draw them away from the path of life? Now multiply that exponentially to try to understand how desperately God wants us to repent and return to Him, so we don't receive the wrath that was already put upon Jesus.

We can store up wrath for ourselves through our stubbornness to God's kindness. Or we can repent, put our faith in the finished work of Jesus on the cross, and receive eternal life with God. Repentance, in this sense, is about confessing our need for the rescuing work of Jesus and receiving His gift of saving grace.

But again, let us not confuse that crucial moment of repentance and salvation with our ongoing need to bring our sin before God daily and ask for His cleansing and forgiveness.

This repentance we are exploring as a daily practice for deeper intimacy with God is not the habitual need to repent so we will not fall under God's righteous judgement—like the kid who gets "re-saved" every year at Christian camp out of fear that the last time didn't stick. That's not how it works. When we repent and put our faith in Jesus, we are sealed with the Holy Spirit and secure in the love of God.

Our focus here is on the daily practice of repentance, through which He revives our hearts! And right relationship is restored.

Our focus here is on the daily practice of repentance, through which He revives our hearts! And right relationship is restored.

Let's return to the parent-child relationship we started with. I am a proud mama to five boys, and because God entrusted them to me, and because I am crazy about them, I will never turn my back on them. Our relationship, and my love, is undying. But when my child sins against me, or I against them, the intimacy in our relationship is strained. I still love my child very much. But right relationship needs to be restored if we want to enjoy connection and closeness. Our relationship with God is not dissimilar.

When I was growing up, my daddy, who was a preacher, had a painting of Jesus in his office. Unfortunately, most paintings we see of Jesus don't come close to depicting Jesus' likely actual appearance. The painting in my daddy's office was no different. But as a child I wasn't focused on the shape of His features or the color of His skin. It was His eyes that drew my attention. Oh my word, His eyes were so tender. So inviting. The Jesus in that painting aligned with the Jesus my daddy preached from the pulpit and modeled in our home alongside my saint of a mom. A Jesus who welcomed me with heart-melting grace. A grace that didn't make me want to grow in my sin but to grieve it. (As you know from previous chapters, this didn't keep me from falling into performance-based Christianity later in life, but there was grace for that too!)

If we find ourselves in the camp of people who say "Grace gives me an excuse to grow in sin" rather than "Grace leads me to grieve my sin," then may I gently suggest we need an experience of God's grace that we've yet to have. We need intimacy with the Father to know the transforming power of grace.

The more I experience His grace, the more I want to follow Him faithfully, though I still fail daily. (That's what we do as human beings; we mess up all the time.) And it leads me to repentance.

Paul explains,

> For godly grief produces a repentance that leads to salvation without regret, whereas worldly grief produces death.
>
> 2 Corinthians 7:10

Do we know the radical difference between godly grief and worldly grief? Godly grief is borne from God's kindness and leads to repentance. It sees His eyes of mercy and draws us to His heart of love. Worldly grief leaves us feeling condemned and hopeless, further from God's heart and deeper in sin.

What a relief that it is because of His mercy, not our morality, that God chose to save us!

Paul writes,

> But when the kindness and love of God our Savior appeared, he saved us, not because of righteous things we had done, but because of his mercy. He saved us through the washing of rebirth and renewal by the Holy Spirit, whom he poured out on us generously through Jesus Christ our Savior.
>
> Titus 3:4–6 NIV

We are born again by the Spirit of God through the saving work of Jesus.

Our most righteous acts and generous deeds fall short of having any saving effects, because even these things are tainted with sin, or with self-serving and impure motives such as looking good in front of our neighbors and feeling good about ourselves. The truth is that we deserve nothing, but He gives us everything in Jesus. Because of His loving kindness, we are led to repentance and receive the immeasurable benefits of His forgiveness.

WORD

Read Matthew 27:27–54. Journal your reflections, meditate on the lengths to which Jesus went to rescue you, and let it lead you to repentance.

SPIRIT

When our hearts are hard and unrepentant, we can ask the Spirit to show us what our sin cost Jesus. Ask the Holy Spirit to bring conviction where there is no contrition. Ask Him to help you see the kindness in the eyes of Jesus. Drink gladly the refreshment that comes with repentance!

DAY 17

What Are the Benefits of Repentance?

If I told you that receiving a renewed mind and a refreshed heart was entirely possible, how would you feel about that? I hope you're expectant, because this is what we are invited to receive when we repent.

We are transformed, mind and heart, through repentance. The Holy Spirit is given to transform us into greater reflectors of God's goodness!

We hear a lot about how Jesus transforms us, so much so that I think the radical nature of transformation gets lost on us. Transformation is not accomplished by simply determining to change our outward behavior, which we all know only lasts for so long and gets us so far. Transformation is something that takes place internally through the power of the Holy Spirit.

This isn't about a better version of the same old you. This is about a blood-bought new you. He's after internal transformation that heals us and leads to new desires and new behaviors. Transformation that makes us motivated by *desire for God* more than *duty to God* to do the things we ought to do to stay close to Him and not be swayed by sin. The ways of this world are contrary to how Jesus lived and how He calls us to emulate Him. It's only by His Spirit in us that we are able to be conformed to the image of Christ.

Earlier I described repentance as a change of heart that leads to a change in thinking and direction. A deliberate turning from sin to holiness, righteousness, and obedience.

Therefore, it would make sense that a benefit of repentance is the renewal of our mind. We decide to turn from our sin, by the power of the Holy Spirit, and set our minds on what is good and holy and true. The Bible is not short on passages (emphases added) showing how this happens.

- "*Set your minds* on things that are above, not on things that are on earth" (Colossians 3:2).
- "Whatever is true . . . honorable . . . just . . . pure . . . lovely . . . commendable . . . *think* about these things" (Philippians 4:8).
- "This Book of the Law shall not depart from your mouth, but you shall *meditate* on it day and night" (Joshua 1:8).
- Blessed is the man whose "delight is in the law of the LORD, and on his law he *meditates* day and night" (Psalm 1:1–2).

Each of these verses holds important instruction on how to change our thinking, and therefore our way of living.

Paul teaches us how renewed minds lead to transformed lives when he writes,

> Do not be conformed to this world, but be transformed by the renewal of your mind, that by testing you may discern what is the will of God, what is good and acceptable and perfect.
>
> Romans 12:2

We need our minds renewed because our minds lean toward "me and my desires and my glory" more than our minds lean toward meditating on Him and His desires and His glory. This causes us to be terribly unhappy people, looking inward for what can only be found looking upward.

So how does this happen? We know self-talk only gets us so far. We don't hold the power to effect mind renewal. But God does! And He does it through the Word + Spirit (the Holy Bible and the Holy Spirit).

In Titus 3:5, which is the only other place in the New Testament where the word *renewal* is used, Paul writes,

> He saved us, not because of works done by us in righteousness, but according to his own mercy, by the washing of regeneration and renewal of the Holy Spirit.

God saves us, and sanctifies us, by the renewal of the Holy Spirit. We are dependent on the supernatural power of the Holy Spirit to have renewed minds. We can ask the Holy Spirit to root out the "mindset of me" and renew it with a mind set on God. And one way we participate with the Holy Spirit in this renewal is through what we already read—by setting our minds on, thinking about, and meditating on Truth. We fill our minds with the Word of God that speaks to our identity in Christ.

Throughout Scripture we see God's holy character contrasted with humanity's history of sinning against Him, which should lead us to repentance, a posture of humility, and praise for the redemption we freely receive in Jesus!

Another benefit of repentance is the refreshment of our hearts! Luke writes,

> Repent therefore, and turn back, that your sins may be blotted out, that times of refreshing may come from the presence of the Lord.
>
> Acts 3:19–20

Repentance leads to refreshment that comes "from the presence of the Lord." It comes from His withness. The Greek word translated "presence" here, *prosópon*, means "the face, countenance."[1] So go ahead, look into His tender eyes and allow yourself to be refreshed by the assurance that your slate is wiped clean, that your sins are remembered no more, and that you are covered in the beauty and righteousness of Jesus before your holy God! The sin we've been holding on to, which creates a roadblock in our intimacy with God, can be confessed with confidence that God "will not despise" our "broken and contrite heart" (Psalm 51:17) but will meet us with forgiveness and bless us with refreshment.

A parched soul will find such deep refreshment when finally willing to repent. I have known this to be true in my life. When I've held on to my sin or simply been lazy in confessing it, I have thirsted for the refreshment of God's intimate presence.

Will you allow Him to renew your mind and refresh your heart with His forgiveness and love? Let Him wash away your shame and let the Spirit propel you in righteous living in His power. And don't be discouraged that this will be the repetitive pattern of your life until you are like Him when you are finally with Him. We will grow, for sure! We will see our desires changed and our hearts sanctified. But repentance will be a necessary daily practice until sin no longer fights for our affection and attention.

Repentance is an invitation to intimacy, to enjoy the personal presence of the Lord! But let's be honest, if this is a new practice for you, it requires trusting that God will receive your confession and restore you, rather than fearing that your repentance will lead to rejection and humiliation. There is a vulnerability and a humility required to engage in true repentance.

Maybe you've feared God might respond to your repentance with something like, "Now that's some serious sinfulness I don't think I can get past. My grace is deep but it's not bottomless. I appreciate the apology and even the remorse, but I can't let this one go. Also, you've come to me with this sin so many times I don't think you really want to let my Spirit change you." It's not uncommon for us to believe God would respond to our mess-ups like most human beings would. With skepticism and irritation. It's only by taking God at His Word that we'll find He comes through with forgiveness every time, giving us renewed minds, refreshed hearts, and a deeper life with Him.

WORD

Open your Bible and read Matthew 11:25–30. I want us to focus on the invitation to rest and refreshment in this passage, and how it complements what we just read in Acts 3:19–20. Journal your thoughts.

+SPIRIT

What is the Holy Spirit stirring in you, or what is He showing you that requires repentance? Take it to the Lord in prayer. Confess it, ask for power to turn from it. He is able to renew your mind and refresh your heart today!

DAY 18

What Is the Fruit of Repentance?

Few things steal joy from your relationship with Jesus like the pressure to perform for Him and make Him proud. Think about the way children say to their parents, "Look at me! See what I can do!" They want you to watch them perform and be proud. This can be a special moment of connection and encouragement, but if the child believes their parents' pride is only in their performance, it can become problematic.

We're not likely to actually say, "Jesus, look at what I am doing to make you proud of me!" But how often do we live that way? Maybe we aren't convinced He loves us and is proud to be our Father outside of our performance. Maybe we aren't sure our presence—and our desire to be in His—is what He loves most.

The Holy Spirit opened the eyes of my heart to the saving work of Jesus when I was a young girl with the good news that I am saved by grace through faith. I was taught that my effort at obedience and good works wasn't what saved me, but that I was saved by grace alone through faith in Christ.

This is the life-altering truth Paul explains in Ephesians 2:8–9.

> For by grace you have been saved through faith. And this is not your own doing; it is the gift of God, not a result of works, so that no one may boast.

But I followed Jesus fighting what I was taught about grace. I was plagued by the performance mentality. I may have accepted salvation as a free gift of grace, but as you know from previous stories, the older I got, the more I felt pressure to stay in His good graces with my good behavior, good works, and good everything, basically. I believed that it was God's job to rescue me, but it was my job to make sure He didn't regret it.

This was not what I was taught in my church or in my home, but the human tendency to prove our worth made its way into my relationship with Jesus. I wanted to convince Him and myself that I was making it a little easier for Him to accept me because of how hard I was working to be good and do good.

Of course, desiring to do good works is good. We love and serve others because of how Christ's love and sacrifice has changed us. But what's *not* good is relying on good works to try to prove we are worthy of God's love and acceptance.

Desiring good behavior (a yielded heart that overflows into right living) is also good. Obedience and holiness are evidence we are yielding to the Spirit at work within us.

This is what Jesus was teaching when He said,

> If you love me, you will keep my commandments.
>
> John 14:15

Keeping His commandments is the overflow of love and evidence of our love for Christ, but what's *not* good is thinking our good behavior earns Christ's love for us.

In James 2:26 we read that "faith apart from works is dead." This verse doesn't call into question whether we are saved by faith. Rather, it affirms that if the Spirit lives in us, He will move us to good works. He will lead us to live and love like Jesus. As Paul writes in Galatians 5:6, "faith working through love" not *for* love, is what counts. A vibrant faith will move us to make much of Jesus in tangible ways.

Paul says something similar in Ephesians 2:10. "For we are his workmanship, created in Christ Jesus for good works, which God prepared beforehand, that we should walk in them." This verse immediately follows what we read at the beginning of today's devotion about being saved by grace through faith. We are not saved *by* good works but *for* good works.

If the gospel has melted our hearts and transformed our lives, a desire to live rightly and do justly will follow. We will talk more in the days ahead about how we live empowered lives of joyful obedience, but for now, let's see how this conversation answers the question we started with: *What is the fruit of repentance?*

Luke records these words from John the Baptist:

> He said therefore to the crowds that came out to be baptized by him, "You brood of vipers! Who warned you to flee from the wrath to come? Bear fruits in keeping with repentance. And do not begin to say to yourselves, 'We have Abraham as our father.' For I tell you, God is able from these stones to raise up children for Abraham. Even now the axe is laid to the root of the trees. Every tree therefore that does not bear good fruit is cut down and thrown into the fire."
>
> Luke 3:7–9

When John said "Bear fruits in keeping with repentance," he wasn't calling them out for their sinfulness as much as he was for their self-reliance! Yes, you read that right! He was speaking to a crowd that wanted to believe their lineage or past achievements contributed to their salvation and kept them safe in God's love. Dependence on anything other than the work of Jesus is false repentance that does not bear fruit.

Who can't relate to this? We resist admitting that Jesus is all we have and all we need. We want to believe our contribution counts for something.

What do you bring before God to justify His love for you and acceptance of you? I tried to bring things like rule following, mission-oriented living, and great Christian parenting. But I always knew my efforts fell miserably short. That's when He rescued me from believing I bring anything but human limitations and need! And He freed me to *keep* following His commands, living a kingdom-minded life, and investing seeds of faith into my kids' hearts without the pressure to keep Him proud.

Remember what Paul said in our key passage? "I count everything as loss because of the surpassing worth of knowing Christ Jesus my Lord. . . . not having a righteousness of my own that comes from the law, but that which comes through faith in Christ." This is what it looks like to "bear fruits in keeping with repentance." It looks like confessing how much we need Jesus to save, sustain, and sanctify us!

Are we seeing how it's not only our intentional sin, but also our trying not to be solely dependent on the righteousness of Christ, that requires repentance?

Paul writes more about this in Romans 10:3:

> For, being ignorant of the righteousness of God, and seeking to establish their own, they did not submit to God's righteousness.

Seeking to establish our own righteousness is not only fruitless, but it requires repentance. We are called to submit to God's righteousness through the holiness of Christ imputed to us! Then to live in reliance on the Spirit for fruit-filled lives. To "resist the devil" (James 4:7) and run from temptation. But we need more than speed to beat it. We need the Spirit of the Living God inside us.

To bear fruit in keeping with repentance means that your heart believes, and your life testifies, that you are saved and sanctified by grace alone. Your sincere sorrow for your sin *and* self-righteousness leads to repentance and reaps actions or behaviors that look increasingly like Jesus. Things like humility, kindness, faithfulness, love, service, and forgiveness.

We come to God with our repentance, not relying on anything we bring—whether promises to do better or changes we plan to make—but relying wholly on the precious blood of Jesus and the power of the Spirit of God inside us.

There is none like Him. He is your righteousness. Through Him, you are made right with God. And in Him, you are a masterpiece made to do good works and produce good fruit that glorifies Him!

Amen? Amen!

WORD

Read our key passage in Philippians 3:8–11 and write it below, committing it to memory as you write each sentence.

SPIRIT

Pray and ask the Holy Spirit to show you the ways in which you have attempted to make it easier for God to love you. Repent of your self-reliance and receive afresh the Good News that Christ is your righteousness.

DAY 19

How Do I Repent?

I have a terrible sense of direction and can rarely remember how to return to a place I've been before. So I'm highly dependent on my navigation system to get me where I need to go.

Today we're talking about ***how*** to repent, and we're going to use Psalm 51 as our navigation system. In this psalm, King David offers us good directions and guidance—not for a road trip, but for repentance. For those who feel they don't have a good sense of how to go to the Lord in repentance, or for those who feel like they've been there before (when you received salvation) but don't know how to return, lean in!

As we read this psalm, let it not be lost on us that David was at his lowest when he wrote this personal confession and plea for cleansing after committing murder and adultery. David, described as "a man after [God's] own heart" (1 Samuel 13:14) fell, and he fell hard. Through David we are reminded that even those who earnestly pursue God are prone to fall. And that there is nothing we cannot bring before our merciful and loving Father.

Let's start by reading the entirety of Psalm 51 in our Bibles. I offer verses 1–17 in sections below, using the NIV translation, but I'd love for you to read the whole psalm first. (I'll wait while you open your Bible, your Bible app, or Biblegateway.com to read it.)

This psalm will guide us to our destination of true repentance. But I want to remind us that this isn't a formula, nor is it the only way to repent. Just like on a road trip, there are various routes that get us to our final destination. This is just one of them. But I think it's a good one, and one that has been so powerful in my own life of prayer and repentance.

1. Psalm 51:1:

   > Have mercy on me, O God,
   >   according to your unfailing love;
   > according to your great compassion
   >   blot out my transgressions.

   David begins by acknowledging the character of God. We can have confidence coming before Him as David did because He is a God of unfailing love and great compassion who shows mercy to His children.

2. Psalm 51:2–3:

   > Wash away all my iniquity
   > and cleanse me from my sin.
   > For I know my transgressions,
   > and my sin is always before me.

   David owns his sin. He doesn't rationalize it or minimize it. He confesses that not only has he sinned, but his sin is "always before him," meaning on his mind. Naming our sin is a significant part of repentance.

3. Psalm 51:4–6:

   > Against you, you only, have I sinned
   >   and done what is evil in your sight;
   > so you are right in your verdict
   >   and justified when you judge.

> Surely I was sinful at birth,
>   sinful from the time my mother conceived me.
> Yet you desired faithfulness even in the womb;
>   you taught me wisdom in that secret place.

David names God as the One whom his sin is ultimately against. Yes, many people were hurt by David's sin. Adultery, deceit, and murder were all at play, and forgiveness should be sought from the people he sinned against. But foremost our sin is an offense against our holy God. "There is no self-justification, only affirmation of God's justice," states the ESV Gospel Transformation Bible commentary.[1] Sin is part of the human condition before we are even born into this fallen world, but it does not have the final say.

4. Psalm 51:7–9:

> Cleanse me with hyssop, and I will be clean;
>   wash me, and I will be whiter than snow.
> Let me hear joy and gladness;
>   let the bones you have crushed rejoice.
> Hide your face from my sins
>   and blot out all my iniquity.

David seeks perfect cleansing and forgiveness, and affirms that God is able! Complete cleansing is ours because of Jesus' blood. This makes me think about the uniforms I wash after one of my boys' football games. No matter how powerful the detergent, there is still evidence of dirt. They're never white as snow. But the blood of Jesus is powerful enough to cleanse so thoroughly that no stain of sin remains. It washes us white as snow. Let joy and gladness fill our hearts!

5. Psalm 51:10–12:

> Create in me a pure heart, O God,
>   and renew a steadfast spirit within me.
> Do not cast me from your presence
>   or take your Holy Spirit from me.
> Restore to me the joy of your salvation
>   and grant me a willing spirit, to sustain me.

David's prayer for purity is so beautiful, and I know God delights to provide us with what David pleaded for: restoration, a pure heart, a steadfast spirit, and the Spirit's presence. We can't pull off a pure heart on our own. This is what God does in us! And He renews our devotion to pursue Him.

When David pleads with God not to take His Spirit from him, note that this happened before Pentecost, back when the Spirit came upon people for a specific task or season as God chose to anoint them. So it was understandable that David feared God would take His Spirit/anointing from him as He did with Saul, the king before him. But because of Pentecost, the Spirit takes up *permanent* residence in us, and we do not need to fear God taking His Spirit from us as David did. Still, we know our sin grieves the Spirit in us and can make God feel distant from us.

6. Psalm 51:13–15:

> Then I will teach transgressors your ways,
>   so that sinners will turn back to you.
> Deliver me from the guilt of bloodshed, O God,
>   you who are God my Savior,
>   and my tongue will sing of your righteousness.

> Open my lips, Lord,
> and my mouth will declare your praise.

David praised God for His forgiveness! God doesn't grant us forgiveness only for us to walk away feeling like failures. Leave your sin *and shame* in His hands. Let the forgiveness you've received compel you to share the good news of God's grace with others. "Joyful obedience—never pride—is the response to grace," the ESV commentary observes.[2]

7. Psalm 51:16–17:

> You do not delight in sacrifice, or I would bring it;
> you do not take pleasure in burnt offerings.
> My sacrifice, O God, is a broken spirit;
> a broken and contrite heart
> you, God, will not despise.

This portion, I believe, best demonstrates why David is called a man after God's own heart. He is brokenhearted over His sin. Sincerely repentant. David longs to follow God's decrees faithfully. He wants his heart to be responsive to the things God loves and repelled by the things God hates. Like David, we can now pursue holy living in gratitude for God's grace rather than guilt over what we did.

In closing, let us remember, repentance is not a checklist. These verses are meant to guide us and give us words for our desire to be washed clean and kept close! Finally, and perhaps most importantly, our repentance need not be refined. As Alicia Britt Chole said, "I wonder if God might view our sincere repentance like we view a toddler's sincere kiss—messy, clumsy . . . and glorious."[3] We don't have to be well-dressed to be washed clean. Come unpolished. Come broken. Come sincerely. Grace is here.

WORD

Read 1 John 1:5–10. Meditate on the good news that "if we confess our sins, he is faithful and just to forgive us our sins and to cleanse us from all unrighteousness" (verse 9) and journal what God highlighted for you in this passage.

SPIRIT

Below is a prayer of repentance that I rehearse often and have come to love. After you pray these words, hold space for the Holy Spirit to bring to mind that which you need to repent of and to receive the refreshment of forgiveness for.

Most merciful God,
I confess that I have sinned against you
in thought, word, and deed,
by what I have done, and by what I have left undone.

I have not loved you with my whole heart;
I have not loved my neighbors as myself.
I am truly sorry and I humbly repent.

For the sake of your Son Jesus Christ,
have mercy on me and forgive me;
that I may delight in your will, and walk in your ways,
to the glory of your Name. Amen.

—adapted from *The Book of Common Prayer*[4]

DAY 20

How Do I Run the Race Well?

Hiking the Narrows at Zion National Park with my family was one of life's highlights! The Narrows is the narrowest section of Zion Canyon. This gorge, with walls a thousand feet tall and the river sometimes just twenty to thirty feet wide, is one of breathtaking beauty. I was in absolute awe as we waded upstream with our hiking poles in hand, just marveling at the creativity of our God displayed in the majesty of the canyon. Add this to your bucket list if you've not been yet!

Finn, our youngest, was only six at the time. He was such a trooper, hanging in there with his older brothers through what was sometimes waist-high water. About halfway through the hike, Finn decided to start collecting rocks, and each time he found a rock that was more impressive than the one he was holding, he'd add it to the collection. As you might imagine, this began to slow him, and therefore us, down.

Finn cared deeply about his rock collecting, but as the rocks got heavier, and carrying them got harder, my husband, Mike, offered to help him. "Buddy, can I carry those for you?" Finn didn't want to admit he needed help to keep carrying the rocks while trying to navigate the instability of the Narrows. "I'm strong enough to carry them. I don't need help, but thanks, Dad."

This continued for quite a while, but eventually, probably around the third hour of the five-hour hike, Finn gave in and handed the rocks over to Mike. "Dad, promise you won't lose these. It's getting too heavy and I'm so tired. Will you carry them for me?" Mike replied, "I'd love to, buddy. Give them all to me. You can trust me." Not long after Finn surrendered the rocks, he surrendered himself. "Dad, can you carry *me*?"

The author of Hebrews guides us in what to do with the things that weigh us down:

> Therefore, since we are surrounded by so great a cloud of witnesses, let us also lay aside every weight, and sin which clings so closely, and let us run with endurance the race that is set before us, looking to Jesus, the founder and perfecter of our faith, who for the joy that was set before him endured the cross, despising the shame, and is seated at the right hand of the throne of God.
>
> Hebrews 12:1–2

"Weight" here is translated from the Greek *ogkos*, which "describes a *burden* or *something so heavy and cumbersome that it impedes a runner from running his race as he should*."[1]

Something that might surprise us about this well-known passage is that the weight and sin we're to lay aside isn't primarily wrong behavior but wrong beliefs. Jon Bloom explains,

> The whole book's exhortation could be summed up in Hebrews 2:1:
>
> *Therefore we must pay much closer attention to what we have heard, lest we drift away from it.*
>
> Pay close attention to what you're believing. Wrong beliefs weigh down your heart, entangle your feet, distract your attention, and deplete your energy. They will take you out of the race.[2]

In addition to identifying our wrong beliefs or perspectives, it would also be wise for us to identify what priorities or pursuits impede our progress in the race. These are indeed all "weights."

We've been talking about repentance as a change of mind and actions that leads to a decisive reorientation of one's life. We turn away from the self (or sin) and run toward the Lord. But to run with endurance, we must lay aside anything that keeps us distracted from the main thing, which is to "know him and the power of his resurrection," from our key passage. We must, like Finn, surrender these things to our Father.

Maybe this is a good time to pause and ask ourselves, *What are we carrying or believing, what are our eyes so fixed on, that Jesus fades into the background?*

I don't know what wrong beliefs or unhelpful behaviors are weighing you down; I only know my own. But I see Jesus with His hands extended to us, asking us to give it all to Him. Will you surrender whatever it is to the One who paid the price and despised the shame? The One who had unimaginable courage in the face of extreme suffering and persecution because He had you on His mind.

What are we carrying or believing, what are our eyes so fixed on, that Jesus fades into the background?

He chose to be crushed under the justice and holiness of God so that we would not be. Now He sits on the throne, with all power and authority!

Jesus is the ultimate example of an enduring faith. He is the champion who suffered and won the victory! All, Paul writes, "for the joy that was set before him." Maybe it's helpful to picture our family completing our hike through the Narrows, with Mike having carried all of Finn's "weight." And in the end, Finn getting the joy of finishing our "race" and the reward of returning the rocks to the water.

It's worth noting that the word *joy* in the Greek wasn't just *any* joy. It was *a specific joy*—that of Jesus reigning at the right hand of His Father in glory, with you joining Him there! We will be with Him. We will be like Him. For all eternity. No more sorrow. No more tears. No more suffering. Only joy with Jesus.

As we meditate on the joy that was set before Jesus, the joy that led Him to and kept Him on the cross of suffering, we will find all the power we need to press on in joyful obedience to Him.

The joy that was set before Him is our motivator "to walk in a manner worthy of the Lord, fully pleasing to him: bearing fruit in every good work and increasing in the knowledge of God; being strengthened with all power, according to his glorious might, for all endurance and patience with joy; giving thanks to the Father, who has qualified you to share in the inheritance of the saints in light. He has delivered us from the domain of darkness and transferred us to the kingdom of his beloved Son, in whom we have redemption, the forgiveness of sins" (Colossians 1:10–14).

Paul teaches that we are strengthened with *all* power (not just some, but all), according to His glorious might, as we run this race, to bear fruit and do good work! He has delivered us from the power of sin and darkness, He has qualified us (because we can't qualify ourselves) to sit beside Him. We are redeemed and forgiven! Praise Him. Thank Him. Fix your eyes upon Jesus.

D. Martyn Lloyd-Jones wrote, "If we only spent more of our time in looking at Him we should soon forget ourselves."[3]

The irony is, fixing our eyes on Jesus isn't our default. Like Finn carrying his rocks, we want to do what we can do for as long as we can do it. Meanwhile, our shoulders are getting heavier, and our legs are getting weaker because we focus not on Jesus but on the sin we want to overcome or the distractions that rob our attention or the idols we might not even know we worship.

Without eyes fixed on Jesus, we run in the deceptive power of self rather than the divine power of the Spirit, only to discover that this kind of self-propelled Christianity is not only miserable but impossible.

Jesus is the author of our faith. Jesus is the perfecter of our faith. He finishes what He starts. He didn't hand us the baton to finish the race by our "perfection." He did for us what we could never do for ourselves.

Our role now is to lay the weight down and run this race with eyes fixed on Him in the power of His Spirit.

WORD

Do you remember what Paul wrote about suffering in our key passage? "That I . . . may share in his sufferings, becoming like him in his death, that by any means possible I may attain the resurrection from the dead" (Philippians 3:10–11). The ESV commentary explains,

"Sharing in suffering does not 'earn' us the resurrection but enables us to identify more with Christ, to experience the power that gave him new life, and to understand more of the love of the Savior who had to endure immeasurable pain for his resurrection and ours."[4] Marinate on this and journal your thoughts.

SPIRIT

Invite the Holy Spirit to reveal to you the "weight and sin" you're carrying, and ask for His help to lay it down so you can run the race in Spirit-power!

DAY 21

How Does God Satisfy My Soul Hunger?

Mike and I traveled to the British Virgin Islands with some dear friends to celebrate our twentieth wedding anniversary. It's been said that God sanctifies us through the covenant of marriage, and we have certainly found that to be true. We've had blissful days and we've had brutal days. We have fought hard and we have fallen in love all over again. We have suffered loss and we have been given much. Twenty years later, we're gladly still learning about sacrificial, selfless love. All is grace, and we wanted to celebrate!

Of all the things I expected to enjoy on this trip, the one I did not see coming was the bread. Let me explain. I was diagnosed with celiac disease in 2013. Before that, I pretty much lived on bread. I can assure you that when I get to heaven, it will be a consistent diet of bagels for me. Jesus and bagels.

We spent our first two nights at a resort before boarding the boat we would sail on for several days. During our first dinner at the resort, we were offered a basket of bread, as one would expect. And as I always do, I declined and asked for a gluten-free menu. But to my surprise, I was told they offer gluten-free rolls. I happily accepted but also assumed they'd be subpar, as most are.

But when the server brought the gluten-free bread, I was delighted to find they were delicious. *Really* delicious. The look on my face told Mike everything he needed to know. I was having a whole moment!

Before I finished the first roll, I was buttering the next. I ate the entire basket of bread—all four rolls, with zero shame. Although this resort was known for their exquisite menu, all I wanted was the bread. I ordered a meal because that was expected, but I was so satisfied by the bread that I didn't have much of an appetite for anything else. Not that the food didn't look tempting. Oh, it did. I just didn't want it. The bread was life-giving!

Still, there is another, better, life-giving bread, offered to each one of us. Not in a breadbasket but in Jesus, who called himself "the bread of life."

John 6 opens with a great crowd pursuing Jesus because of the signs He had performed. As the people gathered, Jesus knew He would perform a miracle of multiplying a young boy's lunch of five barley loaves and two tiny fish into enough food to feed a hungry crowd of 5,000 so they would be prepared for the message He would soon deliver.

Nobody understood how Jesus planned to feed all the hungry people with such a small amount of food. Even the disciples saw only lack. But where we see lack, Jesus sees leftovers. Abundance.

Where do you feel lack in your life today? Do you lack hope? Joy? Contentment or peace? All of the above?

What I most lack in my life at the moment is peace. I lay down with a chaotic mind. I wake with a chaotic mind. I worry about the burdens people in my family carry and about the declining health of people I love. I worry about the world in which we live and the messages that bombard my kids. I am unsettled in my spirit because of things I surrender to God but then soon take back.

I know that the "life and peace" promised to us through life in the Spirit is available to me in abundance. And that there is enough bounty for me to have leftovers to share with others. But this requires repentance, trust, and returning to Jesus. It requires daily surrender of the weight, as we studied yesterday, that clings so closely. Life and peace will be mine only as I fix my attention on the Prince of Peace (see Romans 8:5–6).

After the miraculous feeding of the 5,000, Jesus withdrew to a mountain by himself, but the people continued to search for and follow Him. This is the moment for which Jesus was setting the stage.

Eugene Peterson paraphrases John 6:25–35 in *The Message* this way:

> When they found him back across the sea, they said, "Rabbi, when did you get here?"
>
> Jesus answered, "You've come looking for me not because you saw God in my actions but because I fed you, filled your stomachs—and for free.
>
> "Don't waste your energy striving for perishable food like that. Work for the food that sticks with you, food that nourishes your lasting life, food the Son of Man provides. He and what he does are guaranteed by God the Father to last."
>
> To that they said, "Well, what do we do then to get in on God's works?"
>
> Jesus said, "Sign on with the One that God has sent. That kind of a commitment gets you in on God's works."
>
> They waffled: "Why don't you give us a clue about who you are, just a hint of what's going on? When we see what's up, we'll commit ourselves. Show us what you can do. Moses fed our ancestors with bread in the desert. It says so in the Scriptures: 'He gave them bread from heaven to eat.'"
>
> Jesus responded, "The real significance of that Scripture is not that Moses gave you bread from heaven but that my Father is right now offering you bread from heaven, the *real* bread. The Bread of God came down out of heaven and is giving life to the world."
>
> They jumped at that: "Master, give us this bread, now and forever!"
>
> Jesus said, "I am the Bread of Life. The person who aligns with me hungers no more and thirsts no more, ever."

There it is. Jesus is the *real* bread. The only bread that satisfies. And feasting on Him is so fulfilling that those who partake hunger "no more."

The idea that we can hunger no more might be hard for some to fathom because we are ravenous people. And I'm not talking about food. Some are hungry for recognition and rewards. Some are hungry for welcome and acceptance. Some are hungry for significance and security. Some are hungry for power and control. Whatever we hunger for, the question we each must answer is, "Do we go to our Savior, or substitutes, to satisfy us?" Do we really believe He satisfies?

Maybe we're not too unlike the crowd Jesus was teaching. They doubted and questioned Him.

> Many among his disciples heard this and said, "This is tough teaching, too tough to swallow."
>
> Jesus sensed that his disciples were having a hard time with this and said, "Does this rattle you completely? What would happen if you saw the Son of Man ascending to where he came from? The Spirit can make life. Sheer muscle and willpower don't make anything happen."
>
> John 6:60–63 MESSAGE

Do you see us in their skepticism? And yet we don't have to live very long to learn that when we expect the things of this world to fill us, we end up disappointed. We hunger *again*, and pretty quickly. But when we feast on Jesus, we are satisfied. We hunger no more.

A satisfied life in Christ is completely possible, but only through the power of the Holy Spirit. The Spirit starts *and* sustains real life in us. Jesus said, "What gives life is God's Spirit; human power is of no use at all" (John 6:63 GNT).

The only way to help ourselves is by admitting how much the self needs the Spirit for not only salvation but also satisfaction.

Jesus continued,

> "Every word I've spoken to you is a Spirit-word, and so it is life-making. But some of you are resisting, refusing to have any part in this." . . . "This is why I told you earlier that no one is capable of coming to me on his own. You get to me only as a gift from the Father."
>
> John 6:63–65 MESSAGE

> After this, many of his disciples left. . . . Then Jesus gave the Twelve their chance: "Do you also want to leave?"
>
> John 6:67 MESSAGE

That question is so poignant. "Do you also want to leave?" Can you imagine Jesus, eyes locked on you, asking, "Will you be satisfied by me or search for salvation and satisfaction elsewhere?"

Our hunger is for Jesus. May we remember this truth when we go searching for sustenance in anything other than Him. Notice I said "when" not "if" because we are forgetful people. We will feast on lesser things that will fill us temporarily. Jesus is the only bread—the Bread of Life—that gives abundant life in the present and in our eternal life to come.

WORD

Read these verses from Psalm 73:25–28 below in *The Message* paraphrase. I also encourage you to read this passage in the ESV or NIV translation.

> You're all I want in heaven!
>   You're all I want on earth!
> . . . I'm in the very presence of God—
>   oh, how refreshing it is!
> I've made Lord God my home.
>   God, I'm telling the world what you do!
>
> Psalm 73:25, 28 Message

SPIRIT

What was the Holy Spirit stirring in you as you read Psalm 73? Journal your thoughts, then pray that the Spirit would, by any means necessary, help you hunger for the presence of God this earnestly and intimately.

DAY 22

What Is the Significance of Word + Spirit?

I'm not a sleepwalker but I've slept in homes with people who are. It's wild to watch a person sleepwalking in the night—how that person seems to be functioning as if they're awake. Their eyes may be open. They may perform routine actions such as getting dressed or eating. They may go through the motions, so to speak, but in a deep sleep.

Could it be that many of us are doing something similar in our relationship with Jesus, going through the motions, not fully awake to the life we've been invited into in Christ?

God is calling us into a more vibrant relationship with Him. He wants to awaken us from our sleepwalking into deeper Spirit-walking.

Today we will see the essentiality of the union of Word and Spirit for a deeper, more intimate life with Him. And we will see how intimacy is hindered when we don't value the power of the Word *and* person of the Holy Spirit!

For example, if you love studying and unpacking Scripture, you might tend to overlook the role of the Spirit in your relationship with God.

On the other hand, if you know the power of the Holy Spirit in your life and walk in step with Him, you might tend to overlook the role of God's Word in your relationship.

As someone who spent the majority of her life as the former, loving the Word but having little appreciation for the work of the Spirit, I am passionate about the union of Word and Spirit.

Does that mean I didn't know intimacy with God before I began appreciating the work of the Spirit? It doesn't. That's the beauty of the Holy Spirit. Even when we're neglecting His presence, He's still at work in us.

But when we *do* welcome His presence, respond to His promptings, follow His guiding, and rely on His power, we have an entirely new experience of God. We know intimacy only those who are led by the Word and Spirit know.

Both knowledge *about* God and intimacy *with* God are essential.

We see what happens in the convergence of Word and Spirit in Acts chapter 4.

Peter and John have been filled with the Spirit at Pentecost and are preaching boldly and performing miracles in the power of the Spirit when they are brought before the council and told not to speak or teach in the name of Jesus. This was their response.

> "And now, Lord, look upon their threats and grant to your servants to continue to speak your word with all boldness, while you stretch out your hand to heal, and signs and wonders are performed through the name of your holy servant Jesus." And when they had prayed, the place in which they were gathered together was shaken, and they were all filled with the Holy Spirit and continued to speak the word of God with boldness.
>
> Acts 4:29–31

They not only refused to remain silent, but they prayed for boldness to speak the Word, and they were all filled with the Spirit. Not to mention, the place shook! A sure sign that God responded. And they continued to spread the gospel in Word and Spirit.

We also see the immeasurable power in the divine merging of Word and Spirit in the beautiful story of Jesus in the hours after His resurrection, in Luke 24. Two men are walking along a road outside Jerusalem on the way to Emmaus, lamenting the crucifixion of Christ and feeling all hope is lost, when Jesus suddenly joined them. But they did not recognize Him as He spoke to them.

What did Jesus tell them?

> He started at the beginning, with the Books of Moses, and went on through all the Prophets, pointing out everything in the Scriptures that referred to him. They came to the edge of the village where they were headed. He acted as if he were going on but they pressed him: "Stay and have supper with us. It's nearly evening; the day is done." So he went in with them. And here is what happened: He sat down at the table with them. Taking the bread, he blessed and broke and gave it to them. At that moment, open-eyed, wide-eyed, they recognized him. And then he disappeared.
>
> Back and forth they talked. "Didn't we feel on fire as he conversed with us on the road, as he opened up the Scriptures for us?"
>
> Luke 24:28–32 MESSAGE

Their hearts burned within them as Jesus, full of the Spirit, unpacked the Scriptures that have *always* pointed to Him. The beauty and essentiality of Word and Spirit are on full display.

What the Spirit of God did for those men He delights to do today—making His presence intimately known so we burn with affection as we open the Scriptures. The Spirit of Truth brings encounter. He makes the presence of God palpable. He awakens us from our sleepwalking with Jesus.

The men on the road weren't sleepwalking, but they weren't aware of who was with them. They needed the Spirit to open their eyes to see it was Jesus—the Word made flesh—in their presence.

RT Kendall writes: "We need both the sun and rain to give beauty and balance in nature. Likewise we need both the Word and the Spirit in order to understand God and his ways. The word is like the sun; the Spirit is like rain. One without the other can result in a natural disaster. It has been said before: 'All Word and no Spirit, we dry up;

all Spirit and no Word, we blow up; but with both Word and Spirit we grow up.'"[1]

What would it look like if we were committed to both the principles of the Word and the power of the Spirit, to both head knowledge and heart affection? We need both sound doctrine and intimate experience for a deeper life with God. What would happen then?

I think we would look a lot like the early church. There would be revival, an outbreak of hearts burning for Jesus, and lives transformed into His likeness.

If the last 2,000 years have taught us anything, I believe it's this: Theology without intimacy breeds dry religion. But theology *with* intimacy breeds relationship with our living God. Let's sit with that for a moment.

Dry religion is often about the outward appearance. It's more about looking good than loving God. Do, do, do. Checking the boxes and staying in line. But there is no intimacy when you're walking on eggshells.

If we read the Bible as a manual for "training in righteousness"[a] and apply it without the love and transforming power of the Spirit, there may be behavior modification, but the heart will stay stubborn, and growth will be stunted. Scripture delivered without the power of the Spirit welcomed is a pep-talk or a self-help checklist.

Without Word + Spirit, we will be left with swelled heads and shrunken hearts. We will grow in self-righteousness—the death blow to growing in Christ-righteousness. Depending on our good works and becoming proud of how we appear draws us deeper into self-sufficiency and further from Christ-intimacy.

This reminds me of what Paul wrote in our key passage about "not having a righteousness of my own that comes from the law, but that which comes through faith in Christ, the righteousness from God that depends on faith—that I may know him and the power of his resurrection" (Philippians 3:9–10). To "know Him and the power" is Word + Spirit.

a. 2 Timothy 3:16.

We then have to ask, "What good is our good theology if not infused with the love and power of the Spirit?"

Until we comprehend that Jesus wants our hearts to be wooed by His love and moved to faithfulness by that love, we will be frustrated that our effort feels in vain. We need the inspiration and intimacy of the Spirit to spur us on and sanctify us in the process.

We need life in Word + Spirit. Theology *with* intimacy breeds transforming relationship.

We get to invite the empowering Holy Spirit to invade our hearts as we study and seek to live by the Word. God's Spirit awakens and energizes our spirit and ensures we don't sleepwalk through the good things God has planned for us. He makes our hearts burn within us with gratitude for what Jesus has done for us, compelling us to live in response to God's grace. He invites us into life-altering intimacy with our Savior as we walk in obedience to the life-giving Word!

WORD

Read the entire "On the Road to Emmaus" story, Luke 24:13–35. Consider how verse 32 speaks specifically to our reading today, and what that means for your life in Christ now. Journal your thoughts.

SPIRIT

What do you sense the Holy Spirit stirring in you? If there has been a tendency in you toward knowledge without intimacy, invite Him to awaken your heart, that you may feel the fire of God's presence as you treasure God's Word.

DAY 23

How Does the Word Impact Intimacy with God?

I love the Bible.

But we're keeping it real, so I'll tell you I don't always love making time for *reading* my Bible. I don't always wake up and run to my Bible like I run to my coffee machine or my social media apps. I assume I can run on yesterday's Scripture reading when what I desperately need is a fresh filling. I compromise on spending time with Jesus because I take for granted that He's always with me. So the Bible stays on the bedside table, and I try to get through the day without inviting Jesus into it. Oh, the patience of Jesus when we take His invitation to intimacy for granted!

But I do love my Bible! I love how I sense God's presence in the pages. I love how He speaks so personally to me in a specific passage He knew I needed to read that day. I love-ish how the Holy Spirit uses Scripture to correct me and lead me to repentance. I love how the Holy Spirit brings comfort and encouragement and hope and wisdom through the verses. But even on the days when a passage doesn't pop off the page, or I'm left wrestling with what the Word of God says, I know I've been with Jesus and I'm better for it.

Time in the Word is a primary way we grow in intimacy with God, but if you're anything like me, you oftentimes go to Scripture to learn something *about* God—or to find the answer to something you've been asking *of* God—more than to simply be *with* God. If the goal is to only gain head knowledge or get solutions to problems, it's unlikely we'll sense His withness in the pages. We'll forgo the closeness, which is what changes us. His presence is what transforms us more into the people we desire to become.

When we read the Word, God wants us to *encounter* Him, not just *read about* Him or *get* something from Him. And one of the roles of the Holy Spirit is to help us engage with God in the book He authored.

Though the Bible is a compilation of writings (sixty-six books, to be exact) from forty human authors, they all had something significant in common. They were men who "spoke from God as they were carried along by the Holy Spirit" (2 Peter 1:21). The Holy Spirit is the Divine Author.

I recently toured the Museum of the Bible and I was stunned at the historical evidence on display, not to mention the magnificence of the museum. (Make the trip!) If you asked me how I know Jesus is legit, I'd be quick to tell you about my experience of Him. But what you might find more convincing are the artifacts we have access to today that affirm Scripture was not conceived or created *by* man's imaginings, but rather, it was communicated *through* man under the inspiration of the Holy Spirit. Human authors were speaking what was given to them from God's Spirit, making Scripture the inerrant Word of God.

Do you want to experience more of God's Spirit? Spend more time in God's Word! When we spend time in God's Word, we avail ourselves of the activity, power, and intimacy of the Holy Spirit. The extent to which we know God's Word *and* Spirit to be vital is the extent to which our relationship with Jesus will be vibrant.

Our role is to read; the Spirit's role is to illuminate. He sheds light on Scripture, He makes things clear to us within it, He sorts things out through it. He convicts us and comforts us. He guides us in God's best for us.

This is what Timothy was teaching when he wrote,

> All Scripture is inspired by God and is useful to teach us what is true and to make us realize what is wrong in our lives. It corrects us when we

> are wrong and teaches us to do what is right. God uses it to prepare and equip his people to do every good work.
>
> 2 Timothy 3:16–17 NLT

Our instinct might be to read this passage and engage with Scripture as a book of rules, so let's not miss the sentences that bookend it.

Timothy begins by assuring us that all Scripture is inspired by God, or "breathed out by God" (ESV), which means the writings themselves are the words spoken by God. God is speaking personally and intimately to you. To me. Something in me shifts when I remember the Bible is a conversation *with* God and not a checklist *from* God.

Timothy concludes by showing us *why* God wants to teach us what is true and correct us when we're off track, "to prepare and equip" us for what He has prepared for us. God has uniquely created you with a distinct purpose that He equips you to fulfill through the reading of Scripture. Reading (and obeying!) Scripture keeps us out of trouble and on track for the good plans He has prepared for us in the present life. And for what He has prepared for us in the life to come. He is a good Father and His intention with us is only good. It's intimacy and eternity with Him.

But ultimately, and this is immensely important, the Holy Spirit's primary role in illuminating the pages He authored, is to make much of Jesus.

Jesus himself said of the Holy Spirit,

> He will glorify me because it is from me that he will receive what he will make known to you. All that belongs to the Father is mine. That is why I said the Spirit will receive from me what he will make known to you.
>
> John 16:14–15 NIV

The Holy Spirit awakens our minds and hearts to the beauty of Jesus in the Word of God. His goal is to glorify Jesus.

The Greek word translated "glorify" here is *doxazō*, "which can be translated in a variety of ways depending on its context. It can be rendered *to extol*, *to praise*, *to magnify*, *to worship*, *to give honor*, *to give adulation*, or *to express one's fame or repute*, and in John 16:14, it actually encompasses the full range of these meanings."[1]

Shortly after Jesus explained that the Holy Spirit's goal is to glorify Him, He prayed,

> Father, the hour has come; glorify your Son that the Son may glorify you.
>
> John 17:1

Jesus didn't seek glory apart from His Father's glory. We glorify the Father and Son in the power of the Holy Spirit, but the Spirit "with the Father and the Son together is worshiped and glorified," as the Nicene Creed states.[2]

The Spirit persuades us to pray that our lives would point to Jesus. He makes us more like Jesus through the lifelong process of sanctification. He shows us what needs to change in our inner lives for our character to reflect Christ's. He increases our devotion to Jesus by bringing to mind all that He chose to endure to reunite us to His Father. He brings intimacy into our relationship with God as He reveals the lengths to which God went to rescue us. And the primary vehicle by which He does this is Scripture.

So the next time (and every time after that) we are tempted to pass up time spent in Scripture with Jesus—who is the Word made flesh—let us remember all we're passing up! Let's start by taking to Jesus the things we know we need to tackle each day. Open the Word for sustenance and invite Him to speak. Open the Word and seek intimacy. This is never, ever, wasted time.

In closing, I want to address a question you might be asking or a frustration you might be feeling. What if you *have* been reading your Bible and you *have* been seeking intimacy with Him in the pages, but He still feels far away? Then what? I want Jesus to answer this question for us.

Jesus said to faithful Scripture readers in John 5:39–40 (Message), "You have your heads in your Bibles constantly because you think you'll find eternal life there. But you miss the forest for the trees. These

Scriptures are all about *me*! And here I am, standing right before you, and you aren't willing to receive from me the life you say you want."

Jesus discloses that intimacy with Him comes not just in *reading* His Word, but in *keeping* His Word. There are other reasons we won't always feel the fire— and we will get to those—but for today, let us be inspired to quickly respond to what we read in Scripture so we don't hinder intimacy with God. Even better, let us remember that even though our sense of His withness might waver, His love never does!

WORD

Open your Bible and read Psalm 119:1–24. Journal what God highlights for you in this passage about the Word of God being one of His greatest gifts to us.

SPIRIT

Do you want your relationship to be characterized as sleepwalking or changed living? Ask the Holy Spirit to not only foster greater understanding of God's Word and empowerment to live a God-glorifying life, but also for a fresh enabling to experience the love and presence of God in the Word.

DAY 24

How Does the Word Impact Obedience to God?

It is both our knowledge of Christ's sacrifice and our experience of Christ's love that compels us to live Christ-honoring lives. Meaning, intimacy with God is more wonderful than words, but if we don't have a knowledge of God grounded in His Word, our doctrine will be shallow at best, skewed at worst. Shallow doctrine yields shallow devotion. Skewed doctrine yields skewed discipleship. Neither brings us closer to the heart of God, which is where true transformation happens.

Choosing not to know Him through His Word is dangerous to our relationship with Him. It causes us to create in our minds a false god who affirms our sinful and selfish choices because He doesn't want to hurt our feelings. There is no conviction through the Word when we don't open it. *His* truth gets replaced with any truth we want to make *our* truth.

When we neglect Scripture, we cease allowing the Spirit to speak to us through the Word, which is His primary go-to to "teach us what is true," as we read in 2 Timothy 3:16–17 yesterday.

"What is true" is what's been done for you!

This is the lens through which we read it rightly.

By rightly I mean in light of the gospel, the Good News of Jesus Christ. What does this look like? When Scripture teaches us what we should do or how we should live as we follow Christ, we must know that these "should dos" are founded on and flow from what Jesus has "already done" on our behalf.

"The imperatives of the Christian life (what we should do) are built upon the indicatives of the gospel (who we are by virtue of Christ's work on our behalf). The inversion of this order is antithetical to the gospel, even if it promotes good behavior," an ESV commentary explains.[1]

"Moreover, every imperative in the Christian life is provided to us as a gracious admonition from God so that we might glorify him and enjoy him as we live the free and abundant life we have in Christ—who is the way, the truth, and the life," the commentary continues.[2]

When our reading of Scripture is done through the lens of Christ's work on our behalf and who we are now because of it, we will see obedience as an invitation to live as new creations, aligned with our identity in Christ. We are free to obey God with a grateful heart. The burden of perfect obedience is lifted because we know Jesus obeyed perfectly on our behalf. We no longer strive for a perfect record of obedience. We humbly ask the Spirit to sanctify us and empower us to defeat the continual temptation of the devil. We repent and receive the refreshment of forgiveness when we miss the mark.

Peter writes, as we read in *The Message*,

> This is the kind of life you've been invited into, the kind of life Christ lived. He suffered everything that came his way so you would know that it could be done, and also know how to do it, step-by-step.
>
> He never did one thing wrong,
> Not once said anything amiss.
>
> They called him every name in the book and he said nothing back. He suffered in silence, content to let God set things right. He used his servant body to carry our sins to the Cross so we could be rid of sin, free to live the right way. His wounds became your healing. You were lost sheep with no idea who you were or where you were going. Now you're named and kept for good by the Shepherd of your souls.
>
> 1 Peter 2:21–25

Jesus, who never sinned, paid for our sin, *so that* we might be free to live for righteousness. Understanding this changes how we read the Bible and respond to the call to holiness.

I have a silly story, but one I think will be helpful here.

We spend our summers on Lake Keowee, nestled between the captivating Blue Ridge Mountains, with breathtaking views as far as the eye can see.

I could spend hours wading in the water with friends, which is exactly what I was doing on a beautiful July afternoon when my Apple Watch chimed with a notification I'd received a few days before but had ignored: "Record Swim."

That's when I proudly told my friend Paula, "We just broke our record from earlier in the week! Remember when we were wading in the water for hours on Thursday? Today we broke that record!"

"How do you know that?" She looked confused.

"Because my watch just told me we have a 'record swim' today," I explained as I held up my wrist.

It's hard to describe the look on Paula's face as I waited for her enthusiasm to catch up to mine.

"Jeannie, I can't tell if you're kidding. I don't think you're kidding. Are you kidding?"

"No, why?" I probed.

"Your watch isn't congratulating us on breaking a record. It's asking you a question. It's asking, 'Do you want to record your swim time?'"

Laughter erupted.

"Well," I explained in my defense, "if it's asking a question, it should have a question mark. It reads like it's making a statement of congratulations."

The memory of that moment continues to provide much comic relief. But it makes sense, right?

Record! Or, record? One is a celebration of what's been done, and one invites you to strive for something to attain. It's all in how you read it.

How we read the Bible isn't much different. We can read it rightly, with grateful hearts for what Jesus accomplished for us and for His righteousness that covers us, or we can read it wrongly, with heavy hearts focused on striving to be right with God, trying to merit His approval and attain His love.

Rightly reading the Bible—under the illumination of the Spirit—invites us into an obedience fueled by gratitude for grace and intimacy with the Trinity.

But wait. If we don't focus on the law—what we "should" do—won't we become lazy in our effort to obey God? Won't we take advantage of the perfect record freely given to us and feed the desires of our flesh instead? These are fair questions, yet we see a pattern in the Bible that tells us quite the opposite is true. The gospel gives us grit. Courage and resolve. Strength of character. Sincerity of heart. A heart wrecked by the gospel is not slothful. It is steadfast and Spirit-empowered!

One such example is found in Paul's letter to the Colossians. Notice the gospel-empowered resolve when he wrote,

> Once you were alienated from God and were enemies in your minds because of your evil behavior. But now he has reconciled you by Christ's physical body through death to present you holy in his sight, without blemish and free from accusation—if you continue in your faith, established and firm, and do not move from the hope held out in the gospel. This is the gospel that you heard and that has been proclaimed to every creature under heaven, and of which I, Paul, have become a servant.
>
> Colossians 1:21–23 NIV

> He is the one we proclaim, admonishing and teaching everyone with all wisdom, so that we may present everyone fully mature in Christ. To this end I strenuously contend with all the energy Christ so powerfully works in me.
>
> Colossians 1:28–29 NIV

With whose power does Paul "strenuously contend"? The power of the Holy Spirit, which is the Spirit of Christ within him.

Will you echo Paul and humbly confess, *I was alienated from God. Now I am reconciled to God. All because of Jesus' death. I am holy in His sight.* This is the gospel! And because of this, my aim is obedience as I "strenuously contend with all the energy Christ so powerfully works within me!"

Of course, our aim won't always be accomplished. A gospel-saturated heart is still tempted to selfish and sinful living. But we should expect to see progress. Rightly reading the Bible leads to progress in obedience, not perfection. Progress in obedience leads to less regret and shame, and greater peace and freedom. Doesn't that sound like what we're after?

WORD

Read Ezekiel 36:26–27 to think more deeply on what God says about the heart transplant He gives us. Notice what He says will "cause" us to be obedient to His Word. Journal your thoughts.

SPIRIT

Do you approach Scripture with more of a "record!" or "record?" perspective? Pray and invite the Holy Spirit to fill you afresh with gratitude for Christ's perfect record of obedience that is yours today!

DAY 25

What's the Difference between the Law and the Gospel?

I had a conversation with a young woman that highlighted a common misconception about Jesus. She said she is hesitant to accept Him because her upbringing made her believe that following Him is purely about the pursuit of perfection. She grew up in a home with the messaging "Be good for God to love you! If you want to receive blessing from God and your family, don't mess up!" Sadly, this messaging messed her up, and still causes her to keep her guard up with Jesus.

She thinks Christianity is about what she must *do* rather than what Christ has *done*.

Maybe you've heard "The law says do. The gospel says done." Making the distinction between the role of the law and the gospel was one of the most pivotal revelations of my life. It radically changed how I read the Bible, walked with God, and received His love. It's the revelation I pray the young woman I spoke with will have!

Today I want to take us deeper into transforming and empowering grace, and explore how the gospel of grace propels us in our repentance and pursuit of holiness. Rightly understanding the categories of law and gospel helps us know how to rightly read the Bible, and frees us from putting our hope in our effort, goodness, or progress.

So why should we care about the difference between the law and the gospel?

We'll let Martin Luther help here.

> When Luther speaks of law and gospel, he can use these terms to describe a biblical pattern of commands and promises. In his *The Freedom of the Christian*, Luther explains "that the entire Scripture of God is divided into two parts: commands and promises." Luther's close associate Philip Melanchthon will say more directly, "All of Scripture is either Law or Gospel."[1]
>
> The law refers specifically to the Law of Moses but overlaps conceptually with other commands of God in Scripture. The Gospel refers specifically to the good news about Jesus Christ, but Scripture often contains promises of the gospel (e.g., Genesis 3:15).[1]

The law tells us what God commands, and it shows us where we fall short. It both tells us how to live *and* helps us see how helpless we are to live purely holy lives.

> For Luther and the scriptural authors, the law carries the basic functions of revealing sin (Rom 7:9) and increasing sin (Rom 5:20).[2]

What? The law increases sin? "All that passing laws against sin did was produce more lawbreakers" (Romans 5:20 Message). This doesn't mean the law *makes* us sin more. It means God knows our rebellious hearts have sinful proclivities to break the rules. Knowing the law doesn't incline us to obey it, and can even have the opposite effect. For example, a speed limit sign doesn't make me slow down, but makes me assess how much I can exceed the limit without getting a ticket. (Don't judge me.) Yet our resistance to submission provides occasion for excessive grace; "but where sin increased, grace increased all the more" (Romans 5:20 niv).

> Melanchthon puts it this way, "The Law shows the disease, the Gospel the cure."[3]

The gospel brings healing to our sin-sick hearts. When you put your trust in Jesus, you become covered in *His* perfection. Christ is your righteousness. This is the gospel. The Good News!

So the law is bad? No. The law is so good! It shows us how great our need is for the gospel.

Why else is the law good? It teaches us how to live God-glorifying lives free from shame and the consequences of sin. The law is essential and beautiful. The law, however, does not have the power to propel you to obedience.

So it's hopeless? Nope!

> God has done in Christ what the Law could not do in us. In Christ, God not only finds the perfect substitute for our sins but the fulfiller of all righteousness on our behalf. We are not only forgiven, but are accounted as those who have perfectly fulfilled God's moral will in thought, word, and deed.[4]

The gospel imparts the Spirit of freedom so we are not paralyzed by guilt but propelled to pursue holiness with hearts empowered by grace. While we are commanded to pursue God and His righteousness, our motivation is gratitude to God and our power is the Spirit of God.

This is the Good News that set me free to stop trying to be my own savior and start allowing the saving love of Jesus to be the only thing that gave me confidence in God's love for, pleasure in, delight over, and acceptance of me!

This is the Good News that invites us to passionately pray, *Jesus, you alone are the reason I am secure in God's love. No fear of rejection. No fear of not being good enough. I am found in you. Now I am free to stop worrying that God will stop loving me because my selfish heart struggles to fulfill the most important commandment.*

What is the most important commandment? When asked this,

> Jesus answered, "The most important one is, 'Hear, O Israel: The Lord our God, the Lord is one. And you shall love the Lord your God with all

> your heart and with all your soul and with all your mind and with all your strength. The second is this: 'You shall love your neighbor as yourself.' There is no other commandment greater than these."
>
> Mark 12:29–31

I want to love God this way. I want to love others this way. But I confess I often love myself more than God and others. That's the human condition.

I'm reminded of the morning I woke around 3 a.m. with what felt like a weighted blanket on my heart. It's not unusual for me to wake in the middle of the night, but I felt this was different right away. I felt the weight of my sin. Not one big sin weighing on me. It was sin upon sin—the daily ones that are easy to overlook or minimize but that grieve the Spirit within me, leave me carrying guilt, and hinder me in living a God-glorifying life. The ones that remind me how often I don't love God and others with *all* my heart and soul and mind and strength.

In moments like this I am immensely grateful for what I now know of the law and the gospel. The law shows me my sin, but I'm not stuck there. Rather than endure a sleepless night where I wallow in shame and worry that God might give up on me, I repent of what I've done and give thanks for what Jesus has done. I am covered in Christ. The blanket on my heart is lifted by the gospel of grace.

In moments like these, my spirit resonates with what King David wrote:

> Blessed is the one
> whose transgressions are forgiven,
> whose sins are covered.
> Blessed is the one
> whose sin the Lord does not count against them
> and in whose spirit is no deceit.
> When I kept silent,
> my bones wasted away
> through my groaning all day long.
> For day and night
> your hand was heavy on me;

my strength was sapped
as in the heat of summer
Then I acknowledged my sin to you
and did not cover up my iniquity.
I said, "I will confess
my transgressions to the LORD."
And you forgave
the guilt of my sin.

Psalm 32:1–5 NIV

Notice how, after recounting the heaviness of his sin, David declares "Then I acknowledged my sin to you!" He confessed. God forgave. Guilt gone. God glorified.

Jesus did for you and for me what we could never do for ourselves. He fulfilled the law. He lived in perfect obedience to His Father. We are covered in His righteousness before God. Now we can enjoy every spiritual blessing in Christ, empowered by His Spirit, and sanctified by His transforming grace.

This is the gospel of grace, the Good News that frees hearts and changes lives.

WORD

Read 1 John 2:4–6. Notice John speaks of how love and an intimate relationship with God influence the way we obey God. Journal your thoughts.

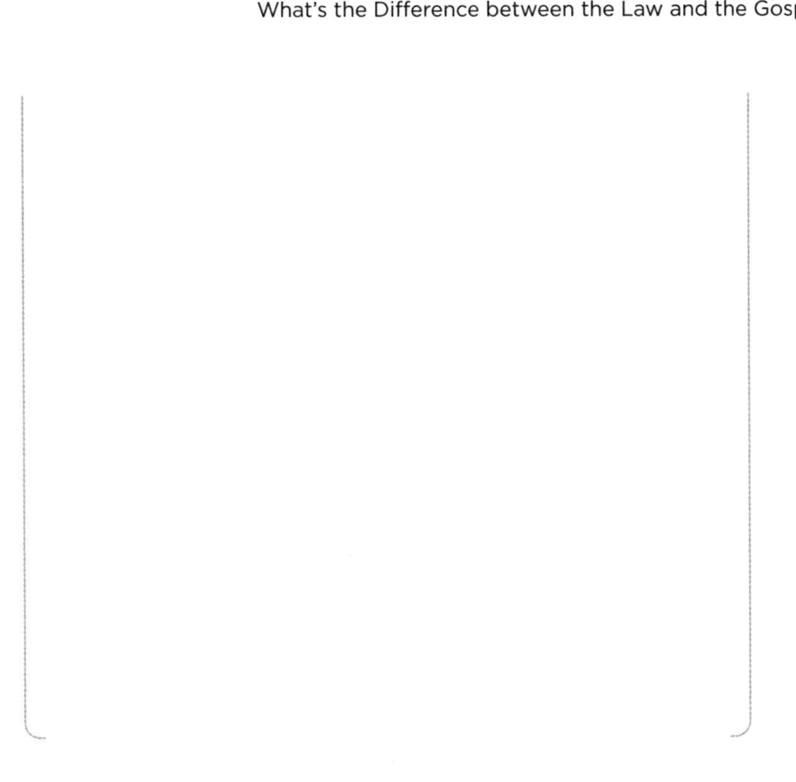

SPIRIT

Like David did, confess your transgressions and receive forgiveness. Invite the Spirit of freedom to empower your heart with the gospel and propel you in obedience to the One who was perfectly obedient to the Father on your behalf.

DAY 26

How Do I Live a Life Worthy of the Lord?

There are very few things in life we don't have to earn. We earn a spot on a team. We earn our degrees. We earn a living. We earn promotions. We earn awards. We even have to earn people's trust. We are programmed to earn. So it can be hard to accept that the most significant thing in our lives—our security in Christ—can't be earned. It is freely given and humbly received. We bring nothing but our need. And we don't like being needy. But oh the freedom our ever-striving hearts receive when we surrender to the gospel message that we are qualified through Christ's perfect sacrifice.

Freedom from having to *earn* God's love, however, is not the same thing as freedom from putting *effort* into the relationship. If we want to live pure and purposeful lives, if we want to be fruit-bearing people, we must participate in our growth in godliness. Effort is essential.

So after several days of looking at how the gospel, the Good News of Jesus Christ, inspires us to walk in faithfulness, I want to be sure that we don't slip into sloppy theology and neglect the pivotal role we play by participating in the good work God has prepared for us to build His kingdom.

There are two passages I want us to read together today.

The first is a portion of Paul's letter to the Colossians that we read on Day 20, and it serves us well again here.

> And so, from the day we heard, we have not ceased to pray for you, asking that you may be filled with the knowledge of his will in all spiritual wisdom and understanding, so as to walk in a manner worthy of the Lord, fully pleasing to him: bearing fruit in every good work and increasing in the knowledge of God; being strengthened with all power, according to his glorious might, for all endurance and patience with joy; giving thanks to the Father, who has qualified you to share in the inheritance of the saints in light. He has delivered us from the domain of darkness and transferred us to the kingdom of his beloved Son, in whom we have redemption, the forgiveness of sins.
>
> Colossians 1:9–14

Paul prays that God would fill us with wisdom, through the Spirit, so that we would live lives worthy of the Lord. Jesus is worthy of our all, and if we surrender our all to Him, we will be fruit-bearing followers who will grow in knowledge of, and intimacy with, God. And none of this will be accomplished through *trying really hard* but by being strengthened by the Spirit "with all power, according to his glorious might" to give our all to the One who qualified us. *His* glorious might, not my own, is the power I am given to grow and bear fruit. Do we see how this is anything but a call to more willpower?

I love how the admonition in that passage to live a Spirit-strengthened worthy life is punctuated with the reminder that we have been rescued and redeemed and forgiven. It is through His grace that we are motivated to live God-honoring lives.

Yet Paul's prayer that we would live worthy lives that are pleasing to God can quickly ignite a self-sufficiency fire in us that is largely unhelpful in what is being asked of us.

Effort is essential, but ultimately pretty ineffective, *unless* it is empowered by the Spirit. The Spirit is given to empower our effort.

I'm reminded of the cargo bikes I often see in our neighborhood. We live in a small coastal town in New England where many of the parents either walk their kids to school or bike alongside them. But then there are the cargo-bike parents. I think they have a secret handshake. I was always so impressed with the fortitude of the parents who were "pedaling" a large cargo bike with several children sitting in the large wooden frame box on the front of the bike, that is, until I discovered the cargo bike comes with electric pedal assistance as an option. And that's when I wanted one for myself!

Their bike had a battery pack. And they had the option to pedal in their own power or take the help of the electric pedal assistance.

We, as Jesus followers, are empowered with a supernatural battery pack. The Holy Spirit. We have supernatural power that energizes our life. And God desires for us to avail ourselves of it. His desire is that we would ask and allow Him to manifest His power in our lives in very tangible ways. Yes, we still pedal. We still participate in the progress. But we don't power it. And when we attempt to pedal in our own effort, without the empowering of the Spirit, we not only end up spiritually exhausted and ineffective, but we forgo experiencing growth that's only possible with God.

We need divine power to do this thing! And the good news is, we have what we need. This brings us to our second passage:

> His divine power has granted to us all things that pertain to life and godliness, through the knowledge of him who called us to his own glory and excellence, by which he has granted to us his precious and very great promises, so that through them you may become partakers of the divine nature, having escaped from the corruption that is in the world because of sinful desire.
>
> 2 Peter 1:3–4

Everything we need to live godly lives has been given to us through His divine power, which is the Holy Spirit!

"For this very reason," Paul goes on to say,

> make every effort to supplement your faith with virtue, and virtue with knowledge, and knowledge with self-control, and self-control with steadfastness, and steadfastness with godliness, and godliness with brotherly

> affection, and brotherly affection with love. For if these qualities are yours and are increasing, they keep you from being ineffective or unfruitful in the knowledge of our Lord Jesus Christ. For whoever lacks these qualities is so nearsighted that he is blind, having forgotten that he was cleansed from his former sins.
>
> 2 Peter 1:5–9

This passage is so rich!

Because God lives in us by His Spirit, and He gives us everything we need, we should "make every effort" to supplement our faith so that our lives ultimately overflow with His love. But it's the last sentence that is so imperative for our conversation. Peter says it's our forgetfulness of what's been done for us that prevents fruitfulness! Our forgetfulness of the gospel is the issue.

But when we remember the Good News, and we allow it to penetrate our hearts, we are spurred on in our effort to live lives worthy of His sacrifice. We are motivated by gratitude for His grace, for our sins are no more. Every failure to live right is forgiven. All because of Jesus! He grants us the right to be called God's loved-beyond-comprehension children. He invites us to live in intimate relationship with the Trinity.

WORD

Open your Bible and read 1 Thessalonians 5:23–24. God who calls you to faithfully follow Him will be faithful to make you more like Him, by His Spirit. As Paul said, "He will surely do it!"

SPIRIT

Take a moment to do honest inventory of where you try to grow in holiness without with the help of the Holy Spirit. Where have you gotten frustrated and discouraged in your growth because you haven't asked or allowed the Spirit to energize your effort? Journal what comes to mind and then invite the Spirit to sanctify and spur you on in those things!

DAY 27

Why Do I Do What I Don't Want to Do?

We took our teenage boys, along with several of their friends, to one of those indoor ax-throwing places. I confess it was one of my poorer parenting decisions. A group of teenage boys wielding an ax for fun—under the supervision of only two parents—is just a bad idea.

The point of the experience is to throw an ax at a wooden target that resembles a dart board, and the goal, as in darts, is to hit the bullseye.

With great confidence, one boy at a time stepped up to the line with the ax gripped in his hand and threw it with all his might, determined to outdo the one who went before him. Over the course of a couple hours, they hit the bullseye less than a handful of times. Mostly, they missed the mark, and it wasn't for a lack of effort. Thankfully, nobody was harmed in the making of this memory, and we shall not return.

Because I know that sin is commonly defined as "missing the mark," I couldn't help but think about how this ax-throwing experience is a lot like trying to conquer sin.

I miss the mark daily, and it's rarely for a lack of effort. I step up to my day like those boys stepped up to that line, determined—by the Spirit—to do well and hit the bullseye, so to speak, with my words and actions. But sin is right there ready to trip me up. And daily, I miss the mark.

It can be so discouraging for us, as Jesus followers, to continue to miss the mark, even when we truly long to love and follow God faithfully. *Will I ever stop struggling with this sin? Will I always feel like a failure before God?* Or, like the apostle Paul, we might ask, *Why do I do what I don't want to do?*

I've wrestled with these questions. In fact, I recently fell asleep praying about these questions. I was talking to Jesus about the things in my life that I know aren't God's best for me and begging Him to strengthen me for even the smallest temptations that don't glorify Him. Hours later, I awoke with a very clear thought running through my mind. I knew I'd forget it if I didn't write it down and it seemed to be something the Holy Spirit would say to me, so I penned these words on the pad of paper I keep next to my bed: "Your flesh won't stop fighting for leadership in your life."

When I awoke in the morning and saw the note beside my bed, joy bubbled up in me, not because God told me my flesh won't stop working against me (obviously!), but because God spoke to me! He answered me. He reminded me that defeating sin is a lifelong fight, but I also know I don't fight alone. God fights for me, and the victory has already been won!

The devil wants to direct my path to destruction. But my flesh has been put to death with Christ. Flesh fights from the grave. I am a new creation in Christ. And I have victory over sin through the Spirit who lives in me. This is the Good News that made joy bubble up in me.

So I want us to briefly look at four things that will help us when we are tempted to do what we wish we weren't: The presence of sin. The power of sin. The penalty of sin. The power of His Spirit!

Let's start with Paul's helpful and straightforward writing to the Galatians:

> So I say, let the Holy Spirit guide your lives. Then you won't be doing what your sinful nature craves. The sinful nature wants to do evil, which is just the opposite of what the Spirit wants. And the Spirit gives us desires that are the opposite of what the sinful nature desires. These two forces

> are constantly fighting each other, so you are not free to carry out your good intentions. But when you are directed by the Spirit, you are not under obligation to the law of Moses.
>
> Galatians 5:16–18 NLT

The presence of sin will always be our earthly reality. "These two forces are constantly fighting each other." The sinful nature is ever present *and* persistent. The sinful nature wants to do evil. We should never be surprised by our battle with sin. The devil is no quitter.

But, as Jesus followers, we know that the presence of sin is not the same thing as the power of sin!

Paul explains,

> Sin is no longer your master, for you no longer live under the requirements of the law. Instead, you live under the freedom of God's grace. . . .
>
> Now you are free from your slavery to sin, and you have become slaves to righteous living.
>
> Because of the weakness of your human nature, I am using the illustration of slavery to help you understand all this. Previously, you let yourselves be slaves to impurity and lawlessness, which led ever deeper into sin. Now you must give yourselves to be slaves to righteous living so that you will become holy.
>
> Romans 6:14, 18–19 NLT

So the encouragement we must preach to our discouraged hearts is, "Yes, I will always struggle with sin. There will always be setbacks in my sanctification. This is part of the human condition. But! In Christ, sin loses its power. It's still present, but I am not a slave to it."

Not only are you free from its power but you're free from the penalty it carries![a]

Jesus became flesh to stand in our place to be condemned for our sin. He paid the full penalty of our guilt. This doesn't mean we won't pay earthly penalties for poor choices. We hurt ourselves and others with

a. Colossians 2:14 reference.

our sin, and there is often a price to pay. But condemned we are not. What we deserve is not what we get. We get forgiveness and eternity with Jesus.

And finally, we have the power of the Spirit. We now live not according to the flesh but the Spirit!

Paul gives us this good news:

> By sending his own Son in the likeness of sinful flesh and for sin, he condemned sin in the flesh, in order that the righteous requirement of the law might be fulfilled in us, who walk not according to the flesh but according to the Spirit.
>
> Romans 8:3–4

We have His Spirit living in us, empowering us in righteous living and growing us in holiness! If we let the Holy Spirit guide our lives, then we will not do what our sinful nature craves. This requires more than praying for power. It means acting on it. Praying while staying in the same spot that causes you to sin will keep you doing what you don't want to do. Praying while staying in step with the Spirit is where we experience the power.

Why does it matter so much that we, as Jesus followers, reject what the sinful nature craves and live guided by and yielded to the Spirit?

Because, as Paul explains, *when we follow our flesh that fights for leadership in our lives, we produce rotten fruit, such as*

> sexual immorality, impurity, lustful pleasures, idolatry, sorcery, hostility, quarreling, jealousy, outbursts of anger, selfish ambition, dissension, division, envy, drunkenness, wild parties, and other sins like these.
>
> Galatians 5:19–21 NLT

Is it just me, or does the "wild parties" in that list make you laugh a little? Not because this is a laughing matter but because the Bible just says things sometimes that I don't expect to read, and it reminds me that Jesus understands a lot more than we realize.

But when we are yielded to the Holy Spirit, He produces this kind of fruit in our lives:

> love, joy, peace, patience, kindness, goodness, faithfulness, gentleness, and self-control.
>
> Galatians 5:22–23 NLT

I can't imagine we have any disagreement as to which traits we want to characterize our lives. Why would we intentionally choose a life full of darkness, regret, loneliness, self-obsession, sadness, and shame? And yet that is what we do when we don't live by the Spirit.

But "those who belong to Christ Jesus have nailed the passions and desires of their sinful nature to his cross and crucified them there. Since we are living by the Spirit, let us follow the Spirit's leading in every part of our lives" (Galatians 5:24–25 NLT).

Friend, I've been tempted to believe I don't have what it takes to defeat certain temptations in my life. And the truth is, I don't. But the One who lives within me does. And this is true for you! Christ in us, the Holy Spirit, is our victory. When we find ourselves once again doing what we don't want to do, and we miss the mark we try so hard to hit, let us run to Jesus for grace rather than away from Him in shame. There is grace and power waiting for us!

WORD

Open your Bible and read Romans 7:15–25. This well-known passage is Paul wrestling with why we do what we don't want to do. After reading, record what Paul writes in verse 25.

SPIRIT

Pray and give thanks and celebrate that Jesus is our answer, our rescue, our hope! Journal the things that keep fighting for leadership in your life and invite the Holy Spirit to invade your life with His empowering grace.

DAY 28

What Is Freedom in Christ?

We gathered with extended family over Christmas break in Palmetto Bluff, South Carolina. We rented a lovely house down the street from my sister's home so we could all be together in one of our favorite places—the bluff.

I woke before the rest of my family on our first morning there, which is pretty unusual for me on vacation. I love my sleep! But on this particular morning, the Lord had a funny encounter waiting for me.

I prepared my coffee and was walking toward the peace I thought was awaiting me on the screened-in porch when I noticed a squirrel running about frantically, chewing on the wooden frame, scratching at the screen, and even attempting to claw his way up the chimney, all to no avail. I'm guessing he'd fallen down the chimney, found himself trapped in the porch, and was desperately trying to find his way back to freedom.

I wasn't much in the mood for an encounter with a freaked-out squirrel. I had visions of him attacking me if I attempted to walk outside and lead him to freedom. But I decided to take the risk because his only way out was for me to open the door for him. More important, I really, really wanted to sit on the porch in peace.

The squirrel sat perfectly still, perched on the edge of a chair, as I stepped into the porch and moved slowly toward the screen door to prop it open for him. His eyes met mine as I walked back inside the house, leaving him alone to run to freedom. But instead of making a run for it, he stayed perched on the chair. I couldn't help but wonder why he wasn't leaving. Did it seem too good to be true? Did he doubt that it was really that easy to be free after everything he'd done on his own?

A few times he moved toward the door, but he never got far before he returned to the chair. He still seemed be to questioning my motives. Finally, after I spent entirely too much time assessing his motives, he mustered up the courage to make a run for it. Everything he wanted, he now had.

I think this is what a lot of us do with the freedom Jesus offers us. We're skeptical. "What are your intentions with me?" we ask. Rather than assuming the best about Jesus, maybe we suspect the worst? Maybe we think what He offers us is too good to be true. Or maybe it's the opposite, and we think that following Jesus is boring or burdensome. Full of dos and don'ts. It's about stealing our fun, not setting us free. So when Jesus opens the door to freedom, we doubt Him, kind of like the squirrel doubted me.

Maybe today some of us are enslaved to a way of life that isn't serving us well. Or we're stuck in a pattern of sin that leads us deeper and deeper into shame. We've tried everything we know to do to claw our way out of the challenging or miserable circumstances we find ourselves in. We've tried to rescue ourselves from our rebellious ways, and we know it's not working, yet we ignore or refuse the invitation to freedom.

So let's look at what Jesus had to say about freedom in John 8:31–36.

> So Jesus said to the Jews who had believed him, "If you abide in my word, you are truly my disciples, and you will know the truth, and the truth will set you free." They answered him, "We are offspring of Abraham and have never been enslaved to anyone. How is it that you say, 'You will become free'?"
>
> Jesus answered them, "Truly, truly, I say to you, everyone who practices sin is a slave to sin. The slave does not remain in the house forever; the son remains forever. So if the Son sets you free, you will be free indeed."

Slavery vs. freedom. We are either slaves to sin, meaning it rules us or entraps us, or we are free from its power and destruction. It's never both. And the only way we move from slave to son is through Jesus, the Son of God, who was sent by the Father to take away the sin of the world.

How, then, does Christ set us free?

He set us free by serving our sentence. We miss the mark; He pays the price. We betray God with our sin; Jesus buys our forgiveness with His blood.

Jesus is the only One who can open the door to freedom because He paid our debt in full. There is no balance left for us to pay. Jesus was crucified, was buried, and rose again to set us completely free.

Paul explains,

> Since we have been united with him in his death, we will also be raised to life as he was. We know that our old sinful selves were crucified with Christ so that sin might lose its power in our lives. We are no longer slaves to sin. For when we died with Christ we were set free from the power of sin. And since we died with Christ, we know we will also live with him. We are sure of this because Christ was raised from the dead, and he will never die again. Death no longer has any power over him. When he died, he died once to break the power of sin. But now that he lives, he lives for the glory of God. So you also should consider yourselves to be dead to the power of sin and alive to God through Christ Jesus.
>
> Romans 6:5–11 NLT

Because Jesus lived a perfectly sinless life, in thought, word, and deed, He was qualified to atone for our sins. Jesus "has been tempted in every way, just as we are—yet he did not sin" (Hebrews 4:15 NIV). Because of Jesus alone, we can be set free from the sins that enslave us and the shame that cripples us.

How, then, do we *stay* free once He sets us free?

Look back at John 8:31–36 again. Jesus begins with "If you abide in my Word." Abiding is bigger than knowing. Abiding is deeper than reading. To abide is to dwell, to "remain," "to continue to be present," and "to be held, or kept."[1] There is supernatural power to stay free when we dwell in His Word.

Christ set us free to live freely. And when the Holy Spirit makes this incomprehensibly Good News real to our hearts, we are not compelled to use our freedom to satisfy our sinful nature but to serve God, and one another, in radical, sacrificial love.

Freedom in Christ leads to a full and deep life! Life with God is the greatest adventure. But not free of pain or suffering.

Contrary to what the world would have us believe, obedience isn't boring or burdensome. Freedom in Christ leads to a full and deep life! Life with God is the greatest adventure. But not free of pain or suffering by any stretch of the imagination. Both "slave" and "son" will suffer. But as sons and daughters of God, we carry in us the Spirit of God who never fails us or forsakes us—and who fills us with joy and hope—even as we share in Christ's sufferings.

Yes, I think we're a lot like the squirrel, actually. There was nothing that squirrel could have done to fight its way to freedom. No amount of clawing or chewing was going to get him as far as he needed to go to be free. He was as good as dead, set to starve in the screened-in porch, had I not opened that door and had he not responded.

Jesus opened the door to our freedom. This is amazing grace. And the deeper into intimacy we will go with the Trinity, the more we will desire to use our freedom to live for God's glory. From intimacy flows obedience, growth in holiness, and life and peace.

WORD

Read Galatians 5:1 and write it below. As you write this verse, keep in mind that the "yoke of slavery" Paul refers to is the burden of perfect obedience to gain God's favor and love.

SPIRIT

Pray and invite the Holy Spirit to fill your heart with gratitude for the freedom you have in Jesus. Ask the Holy Spirit to remove any skepticism or doubt in you about God's grace, and to help you believe only the best about Jesus. He is worthy of your full trust!

DAY 29

How Does Obedience Bring Freedom?

When we hear the word *obedience*, we might think of a scenario that includes a stern parent with an uncooperative or rebellious child. Maybe a situation in which a weary mom is telling her energized toddler it's time to leave the playground. But after repeated requests yield no response, she growls, "You better obey me. I will count to three, and if you don't listen to me, you will be sorry!" All the child knows is that he's having the time of his life and his mom wants to spoil the fun.

The difference between the kind of obedience we're unpacking today and the scenario I just offered is that we're not toddlers and God isn't trying to draw us away from what brings us joy. In fact, God calls us to obedience—to live holy and upright lives and to walk in accordance with how He says life works best—because obedience brings freedom and *fullness* of joy.

Christian freedom means we are free to please God without the pressure to earn His love. It doesn't mean we are free to do whatever we please. While we have free will and can do what we choose with our freedom, a heart transformed by the love of God isn't set on taking advantage of its freedom. Rather, it desires to do that which delights God. Will a transformed heart still abuse its freedom and choose sin?

Absolutely. We can be difficult children. But we will grieve our sin and come back around to repentance and love.

Christian freedom means we are free to live in accordance with our identity as children of God through the life-giving Spirit—and to know the freedom from sin and shame that brings!

And unlike the exhausted mom on the playground, God doesn't rely on anger and threats to spur us to obedience. It's His grace, not His growl, that compels us to obey.

How does obedience bring freedom?

When you are walking faithfully with God, you are not living as a slave to sin—sin that is oppressive and destructive. You are not carrying shame for the things that create havoc in your life. You are not being mastered by things that will never provide what they promise. You are not going to bed with a guilty conscience, living in fear of being found out. Rebellious living is exhausting.

When we see obedience in this light, we realize God calls us to obedience not because He wants something *from* us but because He wants something *for* us. God wants us to have life and peace, full and abundant. (Not the "prosperity gospel" abundance but the kind that knows the intimacy and satisfaction of His presence.)

> God calls us to obedience not because He wants something *from* us but because He wants something *for* us.

Our obedience to Jesus is for our good. God is not on a power trip in commanding obedience. Rather, He is on a mission to rescue us from death and destruction. Obedience is of great benefit to us, and for the glory of God.

This doesn't mean that choosing obedience to God won't be hard at times or won't cost us something, whether in relationships or lifestyle. But it *does* mean we are kept in the center of God's will for our lives, even when that looks different than what we'd have chosen because we don't know all He knows. Obedience often means putting down the plans we had and trusting His. But when we surrender, we discover how small we were willing to live. We experience the supernatural hand of God, leading us in kingdom-minded living. Obedience keeps us from forfeiting the full life and internal peace that Jesus died, rose, and ascended to offer us. It allows us to witness what's only possible with God, to live in the fullness of the anointing on our lives, to walk with purpose for the glory of God. And finally, it allows us to enjoy His manifest presence, to truly know the love of the Father. It propels us into a deeper life with God.

Jesus said,

> Whoever has my commandments and keeps them, he it is who loves me. And he who loves me will be loved by my Father, and I will love him and manifest myself to him.
>
> John 14:21

The only thing that delivers what your heart truly desires is love-empowered obedience to Jesus Christ. And the only thing that can produce this love-empowered obedience is *His* love for us. This is the rhythm of Christian living!

We become more desirous of obedience as Jesus becomes more beautiful to us. His beauty makes us want to look increasingly like Him, to be in His presence, gazing at Him. As He becomes our highest affection, sin loses its dominion.

The gospel of grace, the unfathomable love of Jesus, has always been what woos us to walk in His ways. Jesus' desire is that our obedience would be the overflow of a heart so undone by His sacrifice that it longs to live a life that honors Him. It's *always* been about the heart for Jesus.

A heart captivated by the love of Jesus isn't protected from temptation to sin but is enabled to persevere through it. God's grace, applied through the Spirit, is miraculously enabling.

When we grasp the biblical meaning of grace, we see that it isn't a license for disobedience but a stimulator of obedience.

This is why Paul could write with such confidence,

> But by the grace of God I am what I am, and his grace to me was not without effect. No, I worked harder than all of them—yet not I, but the grace of God that was with me.
>
> 1 Corinthians 15:10 NIV

God's grace rescued Paul, and the effect was the desire to obey God by the power of the Holy Spirit. He said "not I" because he knew it was the Holy Spirit that enabled him in his calling. "Not I" also demonstrates that Paul didn't want the glory for who he became and how he obeyed. More proof that the Holy Spirit was at work in Paul.

How do we know if we are being compelled by grace, as Paul was? Is there a way to ensure that our freedom is producing faithfulness to God compelled by His faithfulness to us?

Paul helps us assess our motives when he writes,

> For if you are trying to make yourselves right with God by keeping the law, you have been cut off from Christ! You have fallen away from God's grace.
>
> Galatians 5:4 NLT

When I am motivated to obey God out of my old false beliefs that He loves me more when I'm good, I'm essentially saying to Jesus, "What you did on the cross wasn't enough." Trying to add to Christ's sacrifice is to call Him insufficient.

So when we obey God in an effort to earn His love or pleasure, I want us to hear Him say, "I am well pleased with my Son, the only One who was able to obey me wholeheartedly and completely. And now that you are covered in Him, I am well pleased with you. Though you sin against me in word and deed, you are secure in the pleasure I have in my Son. Allow that Good News to saturate your heart and walk faithfully with me, by the power of my Spirit, because you are so grateful you don't have to work to earn my love!"

Isn't it freeing to know we don't have to earn God's love or pleasure? Knowing this inspires us to work hard with a different goal in mind.

> Work hard to show the results of your salvation, obeying God with deep reverence and fear. For God is working in you, giving you the desire and the power to do what pleases him.
>
> Philippians 2:12–13 NLT

We are not saved and set free *by* our good and hard work, but *for* good and hard work. This work is our honor, done out of desire and with deep reverence to God. It's done with "*God's* energy, an energy deep within you, God himself willing and working at what will give him the most pleasure" (Philippians 2:12–13 MESSAGE).

We get to experience God himself, His divine supernatural power, giving us both the desire and the power to do what pleases Him!

What a generous God we serve, for He does not call us to that which we can accomplish on our own. Yes, that is a gift! That to which He calls us requires us to call on Him. To be utterly dependent on Him. To be found in Him, allowing us to enjoy the greatest gift of all. Himself!

Obedience that is compelled by God's grace and empowered by God's Spirit increases our sensitivity to His manifest presence.

WORD

Read Romans 6:19–23. Notice what Paul asks in verse 21 and consider your answer. Now reflect on the good news in verses 22–23 and write your thoughts below.

SPIRIT

What is the Spirit stirring in you or saying to you? Consider what has compelled you to be faithful to God. Is it His faithfulness to you? Or is it fear of falling out of His love? Let the Holy Spirit bring hope to your heart, empowering you to live faithfully in freedom!

DAY 30

What Is Holiness?

When Mike and I had to discipline a particular son (who will remain nameless) in his little years, he was often quick to say, "You're so mean! Stop being so mean." The truth is, there were times when he was justified in his accusation, times I reacted in anger and frustration and didn't yield to the Spirit's conviction to be gentle in my response to his rebellion. I've had countless opportunities to exercise my apology muscles and seek the forgiveness of my kids.

But my son would also say "You're so mean" when discipline was done gently. These were times when his accusation simply sprang from a stubborn heart resistant to instruction. He didn't appreciate my explanation that "we expect obedience *from* you because we are *for* you." In his mind, discipline and love weren't friends. He wondered why, if we loved him, we didn't let him live as he pleased.

Maybe we ask the same of God?

The writer of Hebrews explains God's discipline this way:

> He disciplines us for our good, that we may share his holiness. For the moment all discipline seems painful rather than pleasant, but later it yields the peaceful fruit of righteousness to those who have been trained by it.
>
> Therefore lift your drooping hands and strengthen your weak knees, and make straight paths for your feet, so that what is lame may not be

> put out of joint but rather be healed. Strive for peace with everyone, and for the holiness without which no one will see the Lord.
>
> Hebrews 12:10–14

God disciplines us for *our good* so we can *share in His holiness*! It's hard to fully appreciate the magnificence of this without answering this question: What is the holiness of God?

> First, it has to do with "apart-ness" or "other-ness." The idea of holiness speaks to the profound difference between Him and us. Holiness encompasses His transcendent majesty, His august superiority. He is distinctly set apart from us. As one infinitely above us, He alone is worthy of our worship and our adoration. . . .
>
> Second, it speaks to His untainted purity, His sinless perfection. God is morally flawless, blameless in all of His ways.[1]

Jesus is given the title Holy One of God, which means Jesus is "absolutely holy. . . . From the top of His head to the bottom of His feet, every inch, every ounce, the totality, the sum and the substance of the second person of the Godhead is equally holy with God the Father."[2]

His holiness is beyond human comprehension, and yet, when we put our faith in Christ, His holiness becomes ours. This is our permanent position in Christ that allows us to enjoy God's personal presence! But this *position* can't be confused with our *condition*. We still require God's discipline to grow in holy living and yield the fruit of righteous living. This is what Jesus was teaching when He said, "Be holy, because I am holy" (1 Peter 1:16 NIV). In other words, *because* my holiness has been freely given to you, faithfully live *like* me. Holy!

The word *holy* means sacred, set apart from the profane (unholy) and for God. In the New Testament, the Greek word for holy, *hagios*, is the same root word for *saint* and *sanctified*.

As Jesus-followers, we are called to live in alignment with our identity as image-bearers of God, as sacred and set apart. This is a beautiful thing. There is an anointing on our lives. We are filled with God and we are to pursue what is pure. Holiness is an intentional separation from what is impure and a consecration to what is pure.

The Message paraphrase of Hebrews 12:10–14 explains, "God is doing what is best for us, training us to live God's holy best, for it's the well-trained who find themselves mature in their relationship with God."

A deeper life with God is ours *through* holy living!

So when the enemy tempts you to believe holiness is an exhausting, joyless pursuit, don't be fooled. The lie the enemy feeds us stands in stark contrast to the reason Jesus said He came to earth:

> I came so they can have real and eternal life, more and better life than they ever dreamed of.
>
> John 10:10 Message

Of course, "more and better" isn't bigger bank accounts and smaller trials. The "more and better" life—in all its glory and difficulty—is being found in Him, come what may. It's His supernatural power performing miracles in our lives today.

But are we honest enough to admit that we often want the benefits of His presence—the "more and better"—without the pursuit of His holiness? That we want to hear from God, see His hand at work, and feel His comforting presence without the sacrifice of "set apart" living? That instead of submitting ourselves to the often messy but always miraculous process of sanctification, we seek satisfaction outside of where the Spirit leads us. We forfeit the life and peace Jesus gives us.

This is why right living isn't just recommended, but required, for an intimate life with God. We must decide if we will live the "set apart" life. If we want to experience God's presence, we have to pursue His holiness.

Paul explains,

> God has called us to live holy lives, not impure lives. Therefore, anyone who refuses to live by these rules is not disobeying human teaching but is rejecting God, who gives his Holy Spirit to you.
>
> 1 Thessalonians 4:7–8 NLT

When I'm tempted to give way in my flesh, it helps to remember that refusing to pursue holiness is a rejection of God himself. Of course, it's not surprising that we reject God and His ways because we are born in opposition to the holiness of God. We come out of the gate rejecting God. And even after we put our full trust in His Son, whom He sent to die for our rejection of His holiness, we will be tempted to indulge in impure living. This is why it's so important that we don't miss the last seven words of the passage we just read: "who gives his Holy Spirit to you."

What a precious gift. God gives His Spirit to help us live holy lives. The Helper is given to help. But do we let Him? Are we handing over the heavy lifting of holiness to the One to whom it belongs? Yes, it is true that holiness doesn't just happen when we hand it over. But it's also true that holiness doesn't happen without Him. If holiness is not Spirit-enabled, we are merely on a self-improvement path that will lead us to one of two places: ugly self-righteousness or utter despair.

Are we handing over the heavy lifting of holiness to the One to whom it belongs?

In fact, one way we can assess whether we're growing in holiness is by how honest we are getting about how much we need the Spirit's help. This is the humility that keeps us wholly dependent on the Spirit to sanctify us. It's the difference between someone who proudly says, "Look at how perfect I am getting," and someone who humbly says, "Yes, God is growing me but I still see how I need grace daily and how dependent I am on the Spirit to sanctify me!" Admitting how much we need the ongoing grace of God and the power of His Spirit to grow in the likeness of Christ is proof that we are growing in holiness!

Holiness isn't a quest to need God less because we get so "good" on our own. In fact, our pursuit of holy living should, more than anything, reveal how deeply we depend on Him. He made us for deep connection. To be in intimate relationship at all times.

Holiness happens when we confess we are hopeless without Him. So throw yourself on His grace, repent when you grieve His Spirit who lives in you and longs to give you godly desires, and get back on the path that leads to His heart, by the power of His Spirit. Holiness is Christ in you.

WORD

Read Revelation chapter 4. Reflect on the holiness of God and record your thoughts in your journal.

SPIRIT

Consider if you have thought of holiness as hard work to keep God happy. Now invite the Spirit to assure you of Christ's holiness covering you, and to empower you to live God's holy best in His strength!

DAY 31

What Is the Holy Spirit's Role in Holy Living?

It's easy to get frustrated and disappointed in a lack of progress in our walk with Jesus. One step forward, two steps back is a dance I'm familiar with. Maybe you can relate?

Scripture testifies to, and modern-day miracles confirm, God's incomparable power to change our lives in an instant, bringing salvation to a sinner, forgiveness to a bitter heart, or freedom from an addiction. But most transformation we experience is not instantaneous. We mostly grow slowly. The process of sanctification is typically a painstakingly slow one.

But this doesn't have to be bad news because, as Paul assures us,

> He who began a good work in you will bring it to completion at the day of Jesus Christ.
>
> Philippians 1:6

God is faithful to finish what He starts! Unlike a lot of us, who start all manner of projects only to leave many of them unfinished because life is full and time is limited, God brings every person to completion!

"He begins His good work in us by the power of the gospel of Jesus Christ through the regenerating work of the Holy Spirit. That same power creates in us the faith by which we are declared righteous . . .

and by which he enables us to live more consistently with our righteous status by the indwelling power of the Holy Spirit," explains the ESV commentary.[1]

In this "good work" we see the unity and teamwork of the Trinity so beautifully on display. The Father, Son, and Holy Spirit each play a role in our justification (enabling us to be declared righteous) and in our sanctification (enabling us to live righteously). We see this truth affirmed in Jesus' teaching on salvation:

> I assure you, no one can enter the Kingdom of God without being born of water and the Spirit. Humans can reproduce only human life, but the Holy Spirit gives birth to spiritual life.
>
> John 3:5–6 NLT

New birth, and a deeply intimate relationship with God, is only possible through the sacrifice of Christ and the enabling of the Spirit. For salvation comes "through the Spirit who makes you holy and through your belief in the truth" (2 Thessalonians 2:13 NLT).

The "Spirit who makes you holy" awakens you to your need for Christ's holiness, then grows you in holiness. But, as we began to see yesterday, we must participate in the process. We must yield to His conviction and direction.

If we are holding on to our sin, we foster a lifestyle of rebellion to God's best, leading to a life of restlessness and regret. We experience shame and sadness when we intentionally grieve the Spirit of God and ignore His voice that tells us there is more and better life for us.

And what happens when we ignore that voice?

> You are now ashamed of the things you used to do, things that end in eternal doom. But now you are free from the power of sin and have become slaves of God. Now you do those things that lead to holiness and result in eternal life.
>
> Romans 6:21–22 NLT

We don't have to live ashamed and defeated. Now, by the Spirit, we choose the things that lead to new life and holiness!

> Just as Christ was raised from the dead by the glorious power of the Father, now we also may live new lives!
>
> Romans 6:4 NLT

We have within us the same glorious power that raised Jesus from the dead—to live new lives! Not new-ish lives. Wholly new lives! We are new creations in Christ.

The Spirit enables us to live in agreement with our grace-given identity in Christ. We are holy and beloved children of God. I pray to God this truth is strengthening our hearts!

Friend, what are you living in agreement with today? Is it the truth of the gospel or the lies of the devil? What narratives have you agreed with that don't align with Scripture?

Shame is devil-speak. Jesus called Satan a liar and a deceiver.[a] He takes a lie you believe about yourself and hammers it home. His voice sounds something like this: "This is who you are, and all you'll ever be. You are a lost cause. You will never overcome the things you struggle with." He tells you that you aren't good enough to be loved by God or worthy of God's beautiful plan. He tells you that your mistakes, failures, and sin define and discredit you. He tells you you're a fraud.

Oh, if we were sitting together, you would sense the profound conviction with which I write this! I remember a walk I took with two friends, and one of the women shared how much pain she carried because she was believing the enemy's lies about her value. He was tempting her to believe her investment in her four young children was not enough and that she should be doing more "difference making" in her church and community. He was telling her that her past prevented her from walking in God's purposes, that she wasn't worthy of certain blessings because she didn't know her Bible well enough. This was when the other

a. John 8:44 reference.

woman, with great conviction, said, "Oh no, sis! Right here, right now I am calling the devil out! In the name of Jesus, his lies will no longer hold power over you. We will laugh at him when he tries again. He is a liar and a deceiver!" As we continued to walk, we prayed for the Holy Spirit to renew our friend's mind with truth.

We all need friends like this woman, who help us remember what is true—that we are new creations in Christ, *with the mind of Christ.*[b] So when the devil tries to sidetrack us from our pursuit of holy living with destructive thinking, we will silence the voice of the gremlin with the voice of the Spirit.

Do you know you can do that? You can silence Him! Through salvation in Christ, you are freed from the power of toxic thinking. Walking in this freedom, however, takes learning. The "good work" isn't complete in a day or a week or a year. Be patient with Him as He is patient with you, until Christ returns and finally makes you whole. And know that His command to pursue holy living and thinking is about bringing wholeness to you and glory to himself. And it is only accomplished in the power of the Spirit.

Our flesh no longer holds power over us, but we must choose to live in agreement with that truth! You don't become less of a target because you have put your trust in Jesus. In fact, I'd argue that you need the Spirit more than ever. The more freedom you experience, the more frustrated the devil gets.

He does not quit pursuing us because we have become new creations in Christ. But the devil's pursuit of us does not equate to power over us. He has no power over you as a child of God. He only has empty promises and shameful scripts to sell you. Don't buy them, my friend.

What do you assume God feels about you? When this question was asked of a group of women I was recently with, the most common response shared was "disappointed." Even those who said they knew they were loved by Him still felt they were disappointing to Him. If you can relate, can I encourage you?

b. 1 Corinthians 2:16 reference.

He loves you with incomprehensible love. His will for you is to conform you into the likeness of His Son. He knows you will stumble and He is committed to complete the good work He started in you. He will not give up on you. He will not find better things to do or better people to perfect. You are stuck with Him as He slowly sanctifies you by His Spirit.

This truth compels us to pray, as Macrina Wiederkehr writes, "O God help me to believe the truth about myself, no matter how beautiful it is!"[2]

This just wrecks me. I am safe with Jesus. Safe in His love. Safe to come close, confess my sin, and receive the refreshment of repentance. Safe to behold His beauty. Safe to see myself covered in His perfection, lovely and beloved as a new creation. This is where the good work happens in my heart by the power of His Spirit.

WORD

Read Ephesians 6:10–11. The command to be "be strong" can be interpreted in the original Greek in the passive voice. So Paul is saying we should be "made strong" or "be strengthened." See the tremendous difference in believing this strength comes from us versus believing it is something the Spirit does in us and for us? Journal your thoughts.

SPIRIT

Through the Holy Spirit, we freely receive what cost Christ His life! Invite the Holy Spirit to renew in you the mind of Christ, to revive your heart with His incomprehensible love, and to sanctify your life with His presence!

DAY 32

How Do I Grow in Holiness?

I've been guilty of exaggeration to make my point more convincing. "I am so tired I could die!" is just one of many examples I could give. But there is one thing that is impossible to exaggerate—God's holiness. He is so utterly holy that we have nothing to compare Him to! He is so entirely beautiful, perfect, and pure that He cannot be in the presence of sin. His eyes are too pure to even look on evil.[a]

Our sin separated us from Him, causing His face to be hidden from us, and His presence to be inaccessible to us! Oh, but Jesus!

To appreciate this, let's revisit the story of Moses going up to Mount Sinai to receive the Ten Commandments from the Lord in Exodus 34.

> Moses remained there on the mountain with the LORD forty days and forty nights. In all that time he ate no bread and drank no water. And the LORD wrote the terms of the covenant—the Ten Commandments—on the stone tablets.
>
> When Moses came down Mount Sinai carrying the two stone tablets inscribed with the terms of the covenant, he wasn't aware that his face had become radiant because he had spoken to the LORD.
>
> Exodus 34:28–29 NLT

a. Habakkuk 1:13 reference.

When Moses came down from Mount Sinai after being in the presence of God, his face was so radiant he had to cover it with a veil, even as the radiance (or glory) faded!

When he was with the Lord, Moses removed the veil. But when he'd come out to tell the people what God said, he'd cover his radiant face again. Why do we care about a face covering? Because it tells us something significant about the holiness of God, and how good we have it!

Moses' face was so radiant from being in the presence of our holy God that the people of Israel could not look at his face without it being covered. But because of Jesus, we get to behold the glory of the Lord with unveiled faces! "We are not like Moses, who put a veil over his face so the people of Israel would not see the glory, even though it was destined to fade away" (2 Corinthians 3:13 NLT). We get to experience His presence personally, to come closer and gaze upon His glory!

This reality is ours by believing in Christ. When we turn to Him and put our faith on Him, the veil—the separation—is removed.

Paul explains,

> But when one turns to the Lord, the veil is removed. Now the Lord is the Spirit, and where the Spirit of the Lord is, there is freedom. And we all, with unveiled face, beholding the glory of the Lord, are being transformed into the same image from one degree of glory to another. For this comes from the Lord who is the Spirit.
>
> 2 Corinthians 3:16–18

It is in His presence, with a clear view of Jesus, that we are changed, healed, and restored. We are transformed into His image, His character, from one degree to another, by beholding Him. This process is the great reversal of Genesis chapter 3. He is restoring us to the image of God in which we were made—but royally messed up in the garden. As the ESV commentary notes,

> The implications of this are profound. First, we have *unlimited access* to the very presence of God. . . . Second, in Christ we are given an

> *unashamed boldness* to enjoy our free and limitless access to God. . . . Third, this bold beholding of God's glory is the very means that the Spirit uses to bring about our *utter transformation* into the image of God's glory. . . . From start to finish the believer is being transformed by God's glory, for God's glory, and into the image of God's glory.[1]

We behold and He transforms. As we gaze upon Him our hearts come under the control of the Spirit and His character is reproduced in us.

This reminds me of the well-known expression, "You become like the company you keep," encouraging us to choose friends of good character who exhibit qualities we'd want to rub off on us.

I think Paul is showing how this same principle applies to keeping close company with God. When we abide, we begin to share in the traits that reflect the character of God. He rubs off on us, but from the inside out, by His Spirit. Our countenance begins to reflect His radiance as we abide.

Someone recently confided to me that they are frustrated they are not growing in God's character even though they're "trying really hard." I didn't offer advice or get on my soap box about how following Him isn't about trying hard, but I did ask, "Are you spending time with Him in Scripture?" Not much, they told me.

I assured them this frustration isn't unique to them. I also experience it when I neglect to spend time with Him. But when we open our Bibles and commune with Him, our countenance begins to reflect His. Through Scripture, the Spirit increases our love for Jesus and decreases our love for sin. He propels us to pursue what Jesus loves.

See, gazing upon Him isn't as simple as looking to the galaxies and acknowledging His majesty. Yes, do that. But not only that. He gave you His Word for a purpose. We are meant to behold the beauty of God through the Word and conversation with Him. Through adoration and worship. In all of these things we can experience His presence as the Spirit produces greater God-glorifying qualities in us.

Do we know how a vibrant relationship with Him enables us to radiate His love to a world that desperately needs Him? All the wrongs in this world, and all the souls smitten with sin, need the transforming love of Jesus. The deep and wide brokenness in our lives will only be healed as we behold the glory of God. The only answer to all that ails us is Jesus. He has given us full access to the presence of God! Full, not partial. Full, not fading! Unlike the glory Moses enjoyed, ours is a permanent presence.

The only answer to all that ails us is Jesus. He has given us full access to the presence of God!

In His presence is fullness of joy.[b] If you've experienced it, you know absolutely nothing compares to it. On my worst days, when sadness and despair have settled on my heart over circumstances I cannot control, I run to the presence of Jesus. I beg God to let the weight of His glory fall on me and bring me to my knees. And I stay there. I let the tears fall. I worship as an act of defiance to my hopelessness, and I let His presence bring me peace. I let His presence lift my head to behold His glory and His power over all that breaks me. I let His presence return to me the joy of my salvation.

And on my best days, honestly, I just bask in it. I celebrate His withness as He'd want me to. I enjoy it! It's a gift beyond all gifts.

His presence isn't partial to happiness or sadness, circumstances or places—meaning I've been consumed by His presence sitting brokenhearted on the floor outside my son's bedroom door and I've been consumed by His presence when I've been joyfully surrounded by thousands at a worship service.

One thing is certain—there is no better way to live than preoccupied with His presence. If we will be ever on the lookout for His activity, His voice, His withness, it will radically change how we experience each day. It enables whatever places we occupy and whatever ground we stand on to feel holy.

Our homes can be holy ground. Our workplaces. Our neighborhood sidewalks. Our classrooms. Our cars. Behind bars. In bars. Hospital

b. Psalm 16:11 reference.

rooms. Orphanages. And church pews. There is nowhere He is not. Invite Him to make you more aware of Him in all of life, and keep your antenna up!

The more we behold Him, the more we become like Him. The more we become like Him, the more our lives will testify to His redeeming love. This is why we're here! To be receivers and givers of the love of God. To build His kingdom. To be ambassadors for Christ. To give a world in desperate need an encounter with the living God!

WORD

Read Psalm 84:1–12. Notice how the psalmist's longing for the presence of God parallels Paul's in our key verse. Consider writing a few verses from this passage that the Lord highlights for you.

SPIRIT

Ask the Holy Spirit to give you a clear view of Jesus in all the spaces you occupy. Invite Him to make you preoccupied with Jesus, to give you a tangible sense of His presence. This is your birthright in Christ. To gaze upon the beauty of the Father, the Son, and the Holy Spirit, and to be changed from one degree of glory to another!

DAY 33

Why Do I Drift?

Paddleboarding is one of my favorite ways to relax. Alone on the water, I breathe deeper. My heart rate slows, and my mind settles. After paddling for a while, I love to take my paddle out of the water, lie on my back, close my eyes, and just listen to the lapping of the water under the board. I wish I could bottle that sound. I could listen to it for hours. But I can only lie on my board like this for so long because I soon begin to drift. My board doesn't stay in the same place. I wish it did, but it doesn't. It drifts.

What happens when I stop paddling is similar to what happens when we stop pursuing God. We drift when we do nothing. We don't have to work at getting further from God. Drifting comes easily. And drifting is stealthily dangerous. The author of Hebrews warns us about the danger.

The first chapter of Hebrews is a grand declaration and celebration of Jesus Christ as the Son of God. The supremacy of Christ is the strong heartbeat of this chapter. Then we find the warning, as a command, at the opening of Hebrews chapter 2.

> We must pay the most careful attention, therefore, to what we have heard, so that we do not drift away.
>
> Hebrews 2:1 NIV

The *most* careful attention! Not a little attention. The most careful attention must be given to what we have heard, the gospel of Jesus Christ. Why? *So we will not drift.*

The writer says something similar in the beginning of Hebrews chapter 3 about what we must do if we don't want to drift.

> Therefore, holy brothers and sisters, who share in the heavenly calling, fix your thoughts on Jesus.
>
> Hebrew 3:1 NIV

We fixate on a lot of things, don't we? What do you get stuck on? Can you imagine the peace we'd experience and the fruit we'd bear if we just as easily fixated on Jesus as we do on lesser things that carry no eternal value? Can you imagine how close to God we'd feel if we fixed our thoughts on the faithfulness of Jesus?

I think the fact that we drift demonstrates how persistent the devil is. He knows what distracts us from time with God. He knows what lures us away from investing time to go deeper with God. And it's not always some big thing or some secret sin. Oftentimes it just means doing nothing! We disregard the gospel. We believe we can sustain ourselves on yesterday's manna. And then it becomes last week's manna. Then last month's manna. And suddenly we are wondering why we're starving and God feels far away. We feel lost. We might find that we're living with a mind that's always racing. With discontentment that's rising. With sin that's increasing. With fruit that's lacking. These are some of the symptoms that tell me I'm drifting and lacking intentionality with God. That I've made it casual, so to speak. I drifted because I did nothing.

But it's not always drifting that gets in the way of being closer to God. Sometimes it's our wandering. At first, I put these two in the same category, but I see they're quite different. One happens when I do nothing; it is passive. The other happens when I do something; it is active. Wandering happens when I choose to do something that takes me further from God.

Perhaps you're familiar with the lyrics in one of my favorite hymns, "Come Thou Fount of Every Blessing." It speaks to the wandering heart that inhabits each of us.

O to grace how great a debtor
daily I'm constrained to be!
Let thy goodness, like a fetter,
bind my wandering heart to thee.
Prone to wander, Lord, I feel it,
prone to leave the God I love;
here's my heart; O take and seal it;
seal it for thy courts above.[1]

Just as the human brain leans to negative thinking, the human heart leans to detrimental wandering. Without paying careful attention to what He's saying and to where He's leading, we will wander closer to anything but Him. It's what our human nature is prone to do. Shiny things easily capture our attention and affection. This is why I am so grateful for the conviction of the Spirit.

In the way that my "check engine" light illuminates on my car's dashboard when there's an issue that needs to be addressed, the Holy Spirit gives me a "check heart" warning in my spirit when I drift or wander.

He brings conviction for course correction, or a loneliness that makes me desire His withness. He revives in me a longing for connection with God again. He leads my heart home.

Opening the Word is helpful for a wandering heart. Reading the Psalms has made for some of my sweetest times with the Lord. A psalm such as this one helps us express what's in our heart, especially when we feel distant from God:

O God, you are my God; earnestly I seek You;
 my soul thirsts for you;
my flesh faints for you,
 as in a dry and weary land where there is no water.
So I have looked upon you in the sanctuary,
 beholding your power and glory.

Psalm 63:1–3

How incredible it is that the distance we sense is never because God wanders away from us or fails to pay the "most careful attention" to us!

Rehearsing truth in Scripture lifts our spirits, transforms our hearts, and propels us in holy living! Something remarkable and supernatural can happen when we intentionally and earnestly seek and behold God in His Word.

But when we don't earnestly seek God and we start to wander, we need to know the devil's tactics. He will lead us to beat ourselves up, to doubt God's love, or to just give up. He'll feed us a narrative that we're off God's radar. And when He does, let us remember that there is nowhere God is not. We cannot wander outside His love and grace.

We also have to acknowledge a very real tension in this conversation. What about when we're just not feeling it? What about days, weeks, or even entire seasons when our soul doesn't thirst and our flesh doesn't faint? What about the times when I truly don't feel compelled to behold Him, or even acknowledge Him?

I love that we can have honest conversations about Jesus and with Jesus. We don't fake it till we make it with Jesus. We come to Him with it all, even the stuff we wish weren't true or the stuff that feels too ugly to confess out loud, and He welcomes us.

These are the times when we have a decision to make. Will we fight for our relationship with God, or will we let the devil do damage?

These are times when we must pray for God to awaken our slumbering hearts with His love. To not let us stay numb to His nearness. We can beg Him to cause His grace to grip us, and ask that the same submission Jesus had to the sovereignty of His Father be ours through the Spirit. Pray He would burn on our heart a remembrance of the price He paid, and break our heart with the marks of the cross upon His body. Plead with Him to imbed in our mind that we are bought with a price, the precious blood of Jesus Christ. Welcome Him to do whatever it takes to bind our wandering heart to His.

Friend, this is a battle. Sometimes the battle is obvious; sometimes it is not. But rest assured, the devil is never not trying to woo you away from more intimately knowing Jesus and more intentionally living in His resurrection power.

But this does not need to frighten us. If our goal is to not drift or wander, we have a clear path forward.

Paul explains it simply in Galatians 5:25 (NIV):

> Since we live by the Spirit, let us keep in step with the Spirit.

We are indwelt by the Spirit, who is our guide to God's heart! Pay attention to His nudge you feel within to fix your thoughts on Jesus in whatever situation you're in! If we keep in step with the Spirit, He will never lead us outside of or away from God's heart or His good plans for us. When He says go left, go left. When He says wait, wait. Yes, He can speak that specifically to us today, just as He did to the apostles. Or maybe He'll communicate with us through that undeniable sense we feel within to proceed or pause in a situation we are in. Maybe it's through a word He brings to mind or an idea we get that we know is not our own. Or He'll speak through a verse we've memorized.

What a great assurance it is that when (not if) we drift or wander off, God's Spirit is always guiding our heart back to His.

WORD

Read Psalm 86:11 and write it below.

SPIRIT

Make this passage your prayer today. Only the Holy Spirit can do this in us, so let's pray He would empower us with an undivided heart for Jesus, just as Jesus had for the Father.

DAY 34

Why Does Jesus Tell Me to Deny Myself?

In the Gospel of Luke, Jesus gave a strong exhortation on what is required to follow Him, saying,

> If anyone would come after me, let him deny himself and take up his cross daily and follow me.
>
> Luke 9:23

I'm curious what bubbles up when you read words like *deny yourself* and *take up your cross.* Do you hear "Become a martyr for Jesus and resign yourself to a life of misery"? Or "A holy life is a hard life!" Does it feel like Jesus is asking you to deprive yourself of all the things that bring you happiness and pleasure? Or maybe you're left wondering why a loving Father would tell His children to pick up a cross—the symbol of criminals and the most painful form of death. Those killed on a cross knew this was not only the lowest form of death, but they were stripped naked to shame them as they endured it.

I'll admit, at first glance, this isn't one of the more tempting invitations Jesus offers.

Abundant life! Yes, sign me up please.[a]

a. John 10:10 reference.

Life and peace! I'm on board.[b]

Fullness of joy. This is absolutely for me![c]

Immeasurably more than I could ever ask for or imagine? 100 percent![d]

Deny myself and take up my cross? Um . . .

But what if this command to deny ourselves and take up our cross is actually an invitation to a far better life? What if abundant life, peace, fullness of joy, and immeasurably more than we could ever ask or imagine are the overflow of our utmost loyalty being to Him?

The entirety of Philippians chapter 2 describes the gospel lived out by Jesus first, but today we will focus on just a portion of this passage that gives us a glimpse into Jesus going first in denying himself and taking up His cross.

> Do nothing from selfish ambition or conceit, but in humility count others more significant than yourselves. Let each of you look not only to his own interests, but also to the interests of others. Have this mind among yourselves, which is yours in Christ Jesus, who, though he was in the form of God, did not count equality with God a thing to be grasped, but emptied himself, by taking the form of a servant, being born in the likeness of men. And being found in human form, he humbled himself by becoming obedient to the point of death, even death on a cross. Therefore God has highly exalted him and bestowed on him the name that is above every name, so that at the name of Jesus every knee should bow, in heaven and on earth and under the earth, and every tongue confess that Jesus Christ is Lord, to the glory of God the Father.
>
> Philippians 2:3–11

Jesus embodied radical humility, to the point of death on a cross. But it was not for loss. He triumphed over death and the grave and is highly exalted with the name above every other name!

b. Romans 8:6 reference.
c. Psalm 16:11 reference.
d. Ephesians 3:20 reference.

And now Jesus is teaching us how to live intimately with Him, in freedom under His Lordship.

Jon Bloom offers phenomenal insight into this struggle. He writes,

> We keep falling into the same sin when we fail to believe that holiness really will make us happier than giving in again. . . . Every sin is born out of a belief that disobeying God (wrongdoing) will produce a happier outcome than obeying God (right-doing). . . . Habitual sin is not fundamentally defeated through the power of self-denial, but through the power of a greater desire. Self-denial is of course necessary, but self-denial is only possible—certainly for the long term—when it is fueled by a desire for a greater joy than what we deny.[1]

The greater joy, of course, is intimacy with the Trinity.

Let's be honest and confess this isn't easy stuff to do, especially when we try to live this out without the power of the Spirit.

I want us to pause here and consider the advice often given to "follow your heart" because while this advice might sound appealing, it's not advantageous. Following our hearts does not benefit us, not to mention, it's not biblical.

Jeremiah explains how diseased our hearts are:

> The heart is deceitful above all things,
> and desperately sick;
> who can understand it?
>
> Jeremiah 17:9

Jesus offers us a detailed list of what comes from the human heart:

> For it is from within, out of a person's heart, that evil thoughts come—sexual immorality, theft, murder, adultery, greed, malice, deceit, lewdness, envy, slander, arrogance and folly. All these evils come from inside and defile a person.
>
> Mark 7:21–23 NIV

Tell me again why I should follow my heart? Friend, don't follow your heart. Follow His. Our hearts lie to us. His is true and perfect. Don't be led by your heart. Be led by the Spirit. Your heart will lead you astray, but the Spirit will lead—and empower—you in God's perfect will.

In the tug-of-war between following His heart or ours, following His heart brings us what ours most craves! Now it's becoming clearer why Jesus would tell us to deny ourselves (not follow our hearts) and take up our cross!

In the tug-of-war between following His heart or ours, following His heart brings us what ours most craves!

First, He *gets to* say this. Jesus is Savior, and sovereign above all others, so this is not an ask that should surprise us. He is calling us to a way of life that honors His supreme authority. He is saying, "I am worthy of your all." Yes, following Him requires more than our admiration. He wants our complete devotion. (Not to be confused with perfection.) He wants surrender of our whole self. No more withholding the last ten percent. And He wants it daily. This is a sold-out way of life, not a circumstantial or occasional surrender. Day in and day out, Jesus wants to be enthroned in our hearts as He is enthroned in heaven. To deny ourselves is to follow the Spirt in us over the flesh that still tries to rule us. To take up our cross is to be as committed to Christ in this life as He was to us in His death.

Second, what He's asking for is for our good. It delivers us from that which keeps us bound. Discipleship demands devotion and making Jesus our heart's highest affection, because in Him we find the love we have been looking for. In Him our hearts are satisfied and our longings fulfilled. Jesus doesn't want us to settle for empty promises and unfulfilled lives. He knows that following Him is what will fulfill us. He made us and He alone knows how to meet our needs.

Third, could it also be that taking up our cross requires us to empty our hands of everything we're holding? I won't suggest the text says this, but I *will* say we can't carry our cross with hands full of other things. Whatever we're holding that we believe makes us worthy of His love, or makes us useful as His child, must be laid down for us to carry our cross. With empty hands, we can no longer say, “Lord, look at what I have to offer! Look at the things I’ve accomplished and how I can be useful!” We bring nothing but our need and weakness as we follow Jesus.

And finally, let us be sure not to confuse Christ’s call to take up our cross with the expression “This is my cross to bear,” insinuating an unpleasant situation that we must live with because we cannot change it. It’s quite the opposite.

Jesus said,

> For whoever would save his life will lose it, but whoever loses his life for my sake will save it. For what does it profit a man if he gains the whole world and loses or forfeits himself?
>
> Luke 9:24–25

Life on mission with Jesus is where it’s at, my friend. Partnering with God in building His kingdom is life to the fullest. It’s okay to think it’s a scary invitation. We can do it scared. He’ll meet us there. But it’s also the surest thing we can choose. In building our life on Jesus, we will never be let down. We can do it scared *and* sure.

Ultimately, this is about living in a Christlike, Spirit-empowered way that will cause others to say, “Tell me about your Jesus!”

WORD

Slowly read our key passage, Philippians 3:8–11, searching in each sentence for the devotion that overflows from a soul rescued and captivated by the generosity and love of God. Journal what you find.

SPIRIT

Pray and ask the Holy Spirit to help you to have the same passion as Paul, who shows us that a soul sold out to Jesus isn't an unpleasant situation you're stuck with but a gift of surpassing worth! Invite the Holy Spirit to reveal where you're struggling to deny yourself and also empower you to count everything as loss compared with knowing Jesus.

DAY 35

Why Does God Command My Worship?

C. S. Lewis writes, "I did not see that it is in the process of being worshipped that God communicates His presence to men. It is not of course the only way. But for many people at many times the 'fair beauty of the Lord' is revealed chiefly or only while they worship Him together."[1]

When I read this profound quote by Lewis, the Spirit gave me a brand-new understanding of why I love to worship.

There are few things in this life that bring me joy and peace, and rest for my restless heart, like worshiping and adoring God.

"What do you enjoy doing?" is a question commonly asked when meeting someone new, and one of my honest answers to that is, "I love to worship," but I've often been hesitant to admit that because I fear it makes me sound pleased with myself. "I'm such a good Christian that one of my favorite things to do is worship Jesus." But if you asked me for the *why* behind my answer, you'd discover it's not out of piety. It's because I know who I'd be without Him and it ain't pretty. I can still barely believe He rescued and redeemed me. My transformed life does not allow me to stay silent. He is worthy of all my worship because of who He is and all He has done for me. (I should also confess I dreamed of being a worship leader until I was informed my passion didn't exactly match my gifting!)

But through Lewis we learn that it's more than gratitude that makes us want to worship. We love to worship because God manifests His presence when He is made much of. He communicates His presence to us when we communicate our praise to Him. When we draw near to His heart in worship, He draws near to ours in wondrous love!

God doesn't command our worship because He needs it but because we do!

Luke explains,

> The God who made the world and everything in it, being Lord of heaven and earth, does not live in temples made by man, nor is he served by human hands, as though he needed anything, since he himself gives to all mankind life and breath and everything.
>
> Acts 17:24–25

A human's pursuit of praise and approval is rooted in weakness, insecurity, and self-obsession. We crave others' worship to make us feel worthy.

But it is not so with God. His command to praise is rooted in selfless love. We're not doing God any favors when we praise Him. He doesn't have an ego that needs to be stroked. He doesn't welcome our worship because He lacks something within himself. Rather, He *allows* us to worship Him out of the abundance of who He is.

He knows that His love validates us, so He puts His Spirit in us to awaken us to His incomparable beauty and His infinite splendor. His Spirit stirs within us affection and adoration that erupts in joyful celebration. He does more than let us have His love; He makes it experiential, enjoyable, and oftentimes even enthralling.

Lewis explains it this way:

> I think we delight to praise what we enjoy because the praise not merely expresses but completes the enjoyment; it is its appointed consummation. It is not out of compliment that lovers keep on telling one another how beautiful they are; the delight is incomplete till it is expressed. It

> is frustrating to have discovered a new author and not to be able to tell anyone how good he is; to come suddenly, at the turn of the road, upon some mountain valley of unexpected grandeur and then to have to keep silent because the people with you care for it no more than for a tin can in the ditch; to hear a good joke and find no one to share it with.[2]

It makes so much sense, doesn't it? There is something about communicating our praise that compounds our joy!

Sam Storms writes,

> If my satisfaction in God is incomplete until expressed in praise of him for satisfying me with himself . . . then God's effort to elicit my worship . . . is both the most loving thing he could possibly do for me and the most glorifying thing he could possibly do for himself. For in my gladness in him . . . is his glory in me.[3]

This is *why* we worship. But we also need to know *how* we are to worship.

Jesus tells us,

> Yet a time is coming and has now come when the true worshipers will worship the Father in the Spirit and in truth, for they are the kind of worshipers the Father seeks. God is spirit, and his worshipers must worship in the Spirit and in truth.
>
> John 4:23–24 NIV

True worshipers, the kind the Father seeks, worship in Spirit *and* in truth. Jesus is the Truth and "the word of truth, the gospel."[a] Genuine worship that God seeks is quickened by God's Spirit. Our adoration is birthed from our spirit being awakened and made tender *to* God's Spirit, *by* God's Spirit. True worship, then, engages both my head and my heart. It's rooted in sound doctrine *and* strong affection. It's saturated in Spirit and Truth.

a. Colossians 1:5 reference.

We all know that worship happens at church on Sunday morning. But do we also know it's meant to happen in places like our living room, on our walks, and in our cars? Oh, don't be surprised if you see me driving with one hand on the wheel and one hand held high.

Speaking of hands held high, if so many verses[b] speak of lifting our hands as a physical response in praise, why is this often seen as dramatic or uncomfortable in our services? We raise our arms at concerts, celebrating the artist or the experience. We raise our arms at football games, cheering for our team or our child. So why wouldn't we lift our arms as a natural response to our joy when we sing to our Savior?

True worship engages both my head and my heart. It's rooted in sound doctrine *and* strong affection. It's saturated in Spirit and Truth.

The internal delight I experience when I worship Jesus oftentimes demands an external response. My arms cannot *not* reach for Him.

Ultimately, the heart of the matter isn't whether we lift our arms or not. It's about the posture of our heart. This is really important to talk about.

Lifted hands signify surrender. Lifted hands signify dependency. But that doesn't mean the man with his hands in his pockets isn't equally surrendered to and dependent on God. God has no interest in performative worship. But I beg us not to fear looking foolish if He stirs in our spirit a strong affection for God that moves us to physically respond. Don't quench the Spirit's presence out of fear or false doctrine!

One thing is sure: We are all worshipers. Not feeling inclined to lift our voices (or hands) doesn't mean we aren't worshipers. We are born wanting to worship something or someone. Look at how we glorify athletes, musicians, politicians, and anyone else with power and a platform. But there is only One who is worthy, and it behooves us to worship Him, even when we don't want to. This isn't the same as faking it to

b. Psalms 63:4; 141:1–2; 28:1; 134:2, and Lamentations 3:41, for example.

appear faithful. Jesus was clear on how he feels when our mouth is filled with worship and our heart is not (Matthew 15:7–8 reference). Playing religion with an unrepentant heart isn't what He's after. That's hypocrisy.

No, this is about worship becoming warfare, an exercise of will. It's telling our doubting or discouraged heart what is true. That is often precisely what I'm doing when my hand is extended through the sunroof in my car or my knees are on my kitchen floor. It's warfare. It's me making the devil pay for what he's done or trying to do by proclaiming the authority of Christ.

When we praise God, we give Him rightful priority. When we adore Him, we are awakened to His presence. When we incline our hearts to Him, intimacy is fostered.

As Lewis wrote, "The Scotch catechism says that man's chief end is 'to glorify God and enjoy Him forever.' But we shall then know that these are the same thing. Fully to enjoy is to glorify. In commanding us to glorify Him, God is inviting us to enjoy Him."[4]

WORD

Read Psalm 145 aloud. Declare your worship as you read. Write what God highlights for you.

SPIRIT

Pray and invite the Holy Spirit to show you why you have been hesitant to worship, or neglectful of worship. Invite Him to stir in you holy fervor for going deeper into God's presence and enjoying greater intimacy with Him through worship and adoration. Turn on a worship playlist and lift your heart, and maybe even your hands, to Him!

DAY 36

How Does the Holy Spirit Fill Me?

My friend has a funny little sign on her kitchen desk that reads, "I'm just sittin' here, silently correcting your grammar." Every time I see it, I'm transported back to my childhood with my dad who, as a preacher (aka communicator), would correct me anytime I said something grammatically incorrect, such as "Me and my friends" rather than "My friends and I." "Grammar matters," he would say. Now I annoy my own children with the same correction my dad once gave me. I trust one day they'll thank me as I now thank him.

Well, today's passage—just one short sentence—is one in which grammar matters. A lot.

In Ephesians 5:18, Paul writes, "be filled with the Spirit."

The Greek for "be filled" is *plerousthe.* A literal translation would read something like "be being kept filled."[1]

This sentence is the exclamation point on Paul's teaching up to this point on how to be imitators of Christ. He's imploring believers to allow the Holy Spirit, who lives in them, to empower them to live transformed lives as new creations in Christ.

And here's why the grammar matters.

First, it is an imperative, a command. It's not a suggestion. To live the Christian life, we need the power of Christ, which is the Holy Spirit in us. Paul knows that they, and we, cannot live a transformed life without the power of Christ.

Second, the command is plural, meaning he's addressing everyone who has embraced and received Christ. He's not speaking to just leaders and teachers, or to only those who feel comfortable being filled. He's speaking to every Jesus-follower.

Third, he speaks in the passive voice, which means it's something that happens *to* you. This isn't something you do; this is something God does *to* you. You are the recipient.

Finally, Paul is speaking in the perfect present, which means that to "be filled" should happen in the present, completely and fully. It can be read, then, as "Be being kept filled."

To sum it up: All believers are called to be continuously filled by, and under the control of, the Spirit of God.

If you have put your trust in Christ, God has put His Spirit in you. And God did not give you a mere portion of His Spirit. He didn't give you 50 percent at the moment of your salvation to keep you striving for the other 50 percent when you hit a new level of faithfulness. "For the one whom God has sent speaks the words of God, for God gives the Spirit without limit" (John 3:34 NIV).

The Message paraphrase explains it like this:

> The One [Jesus] that God sent speaks God's words. And don't think he rations out the Spirit in bits and pieces. The Father loves the Son extravagantly. He turned everything over to him so he could give it away—a lavish distribution of gifts. That is why whoever accepts and trusts the Son gets in on everything, life complete and forever!
>
> John 3:34 MESSAGE

God gave you all of His Spirit when you put your trust in Jesus. But have you given the Spirit access to all of your spirit?

I hadn't. It wasn't until I'd been following Jesus for decades that I realized I had *all* of the Holy Spirit, but the Holy Spirit didn't have *all* of me.

It's also important to mention that to "be being kept filled" with the Spirit is not the same as being indwelt with the Spirit.

Paul explains:

> You are not in the flesh but in the Spirit, if indeed the Spirit of God dwells in you. But if anyone does not have the Spirit of Christ, he does not belong to him. And if Christ is in you, though the body is dead because of sin, yet the spirit is alive because of righteousness.
>
> Romans 8:9–10

If you have received, by grace through faith, Jesus as Savior and Lord, you have all of the Holy Spirit, you are baptized in the Spirit*[a] and you are sealed with the Spirit.[b] So Paul is not commanding us to go get what we don't already have. Rather, he commands us to let what we have, or better said, *who* we have, have all of us!

There is great mystery—and many wonky illustrations—about how we are to "be being kept filled" with the Holy Spirit, which can lead us to wonder if the Holy Spirit is like water in a pitcher or gas in a tank. While these are intended to be helpful illustrations, they fall terribly short of Paul's intended teaching. There is no faucet to turn on or gas station to pull up to for us to receive the Spirit's filling because we are on "empty." He doesn't deplete.

Maybe this conversation is creating curiosity in you as it did in me: *So, if I am to keep being filled afresh with the Spirit, what does that look like? We sing songs that beg the Holy Spirit to come in power and fill us, but how does it actually happen if He doesn't deplete? What are we supposed to do, since we possess all of the Holy Spirit when we repent and believe, and Paul's command isn't to acquire something we don't already have?*

One way to think about this might be to imagine you are a snow globe and the Spirit is the snow in you. The snow settles until it is activated. Without someone shaking it, the snow stays in the globe but the benefits of it being there aren't fully enjoyed.

a. 1 Corinthians 12:13 reference.

b. Ephesians 1:13 reference.

This analogy also falls short, however, because the Holy Spirit isn't constrained by you. You and I don't control the Holy Spirit. Just because you don't activate His activity in you like you would the snow in the globe does not mean He is not at work as your Helper. But if you aren't inviting the Spirit to fill you, empower you, and invade all of your life, you miss out on so much of what He is given to do! If you aren't making yourself available to Him, you can grieve Him and diminish the sense of His presence or quench Him by not fanning the flame of His fire, but He is *still* God the Holy Spirit in you!

Do we want to know more of God's power and personal presence in us? When we awake in the morning, let's ask the Holy Spirit to fill us, to lead us in God's truth, and to strengthen us for battle that is not against flesh and blood. He delights to make His presence and power known to us as we go through our day. Be kept being filled. And if you need to shake your body a little when you awake as an outward sign of an inward reality, like the snow globe, go for it!

But there's more to the command to be being kept filled. Paul's teaching is immensely helpful here. He writes,

> Let the word of Christ dwell in you richly, teaching and admonishing one another in all wisdom, singing psalms and hymns and spiritual songs, with thankfulness in your hearts to God.
>
> Colossians 3:16

The command "be filled with the Spirit" leads us to "Let the word of Christ richly dwell within you." Think of this as a metaphor. The measure in which we are filled with the Spirit is the measure in which we are feasting on the Word.

Dwelling in the Word and dabbling in it are very different things. Dabbling won't cut it if we want to live Spirit-filled and Spirit-empowered lives. To let the Word of Christ richly *dwell* within us means letting the Word of Christ deeply and thoroughly abide, settle, and make its home in us.

The benefits of "being kept filled" are vast. We'll keep this conversation going tomorrow because there is still much to discover, but for today let us remember and celebrate that this is not something we can accomplish on our own. God fills us with more of himself. He delights to dwell in us as His temple. To make us holy as He is holy. We never have to fear that we have depleted Him. His Spirit, which He gives without measure, is our constant Helper!

WORD

Read 1 Corinthians 1:12–13. For those of you who want to better understand the "baptism" language where I placed an asterisk, I offer this brief teaching. Paul is speaking about *all* believers when he said, "we were all baptized into one body." Meaning, we can rightly say that all Christians have experienced the baptism *of* the Holy Spirit because Paul is referring to how the Spirit unites us to Jesus and His body, the church. This baptism is a theological reality.

SPIRIT

I shared earlier how, for decades, I had all of the Holy Spirit but the Spirit didn't have all of me. Does this resonate with you? Journal what the Spirit is saying to you or stirring in you. Please don't turn the page until you've taken inventory. Invite Him to invade every inch of your life with His presence and power, to fully fill you.

DAY 37

What If I Don't Feel His Filling?

It's natural to think we can equate the Holy Spirit's filling with some kind of feeling. And it's easy to get discouraged when we don't feel His filling. It can leave us asking a lot of questions that distract us from functioning in His power. This is why I'm excited about what God has for us in today's reading!

What we'll discover today is that you know you're filled and functioning from His power when you experience the supernatural enabling He gives and your life bears evidence of it. Of course, the enabling and evidence aren't typically mountaintop or monumental experiences.

We are told to keep being filled because we are meant to keep relying on His indwelling power so we know His presence even in the familiar rhythm of our day. His enabling is for our everyday lives. Sitting at your desk, you can ask for His presence to fill you, and joy can break in. Driving your car, you can cry out to God with what breaks your heart, and hope can fill you afresh. Falling asleep at night with an anxious mind, you can plead for God to fill you so His peace that passes understanding floods you.

Sometimes you will physically feel His filling, sometimes you will feel the effect of His filling, and sometimes you will feel . . . nothing. You will sometimes have to trust that though there was no feeling, there was filling. He will not withhold himself from you. But—and oh how important this *but* is—you may withhold yourself from Him. Meaning, we can ask to be filled and refreshed all day long, but if we are intentionally pursuing a life of rebellion and sin, we can forfeit the feeling or effect of His presence. But when we repent and ask for His filling from a pure heart, we will see just how aware we can be of God living in us and letting us enjoy His companionship and provision.

His presence brings hope for all that feels lost. It produces selflessness, even for those hardest to love. It provides peace that passes comprehension in our turmoil and heartache, and bubbles up joy from deep within that is not reliant on circumstances. His presence moves us to forgive those who have hurt us, and makes us people marked by patience, kindness, and goodness. His presence empowers us to exercise control over our flesh. And His presence—when we are not intentionally grieving Him—produces greater intimacy and felt connection with God!

So asking to be filled again and again is like asking to experience and emanate the *effect* of His presence.

As we began to discuss yesterday, it's right and good to pray and sing, "Fill me with your presence. Fill me with your power. Pour out your Spirit!" Jesus teaches the disciples to do this just after He teaches them what we call The Lord's Prayer.

Jesus says,

> Don't bargain with God. Be direct. Ask for what you need. This is not a cat-and-mouse, hide-and-seek game we're in. If your little boy asks for a serving of fish, do you scare him with a live snake on his plate? If your little girl asks for an egg, do you trick her with a spider? As bad as you are, you wouldn't think of such a thing—you're at least decent to your own children. And don't you think the Father who conceived you in love will give the Holy Spirit when you ask him?
>
> Luke 11:10–13 MESSAGE

The ESV translation states, "How much more will the heavenly Father give the Holy Spirit to those who ask him!" How much? Without limit! And this happens through asking.

But if *asking* to be filled is not accompanied by *opening our Bible* and allowing Him to richly dwell in us through His authoritative Word, we have to wonder if our prayer is more lip service than heart desire, which results in our missing out on so much of what God desires to do in us and through us.

If we say "my heart is open" but we don't open His Word, can we expect to experience the fullness of His presence?

"Without immersion in God's words, our prayers may not be merely limited and shallow but also untethered from reality. We may be responding not to the real God but to what we wish God and life to be like," writes Timothy Keller.[1]

If we say "my heart is open" but we don't open His Word, can we expect to experience the fullness of His presence?

The Word and prayer (talking *with* God) are essential to the filled and flourishing life.

When we are allowing the Word to richly dwell within us, when our motives for being filled are aligned with what brings Him glory, and when we seek Him sincerely, we will be filled. But as we said earlier, we won't always feel His filling. The proof of filling is not in the feeling but in the fruit!

And when God *does* allow us to experience a superabundance of His presence, remember it serves a purpose! The supernatural breaking in is meant to not only fill us but to fuel us in obedience. For example, there have been very distinct and precious times when I have physically felt the Spirit filling me and ministering to my spirit. And each time, His presence brought an inexplicable longing to pour my life out for Him again and again. Whether I needed courage for something to which He was calling me but I was resisting, or He was compelling me to a life of greater compassion in a situation, or He was enabling me to turn from habitual sin that I was striving to overcome, the superabundance of His presence didn't leave me the same. But more often than not, His filling has been unfelt. Yet I know unfelt filling is still untapped power.

Count on His faithfulness to fill you with himself. Ask and keep asking. But also respond and keep responding. When we request to be filled, we must also have a heart willing to be led.

We might need to ask ourselves, *Why do I want to be filled with the Spirit of God?* Could it be true that I want to enjoy His presence but I don't want to live by His principles? Is it possible that I want His power not because I want to better live for His glory but to better achieve my goals? Do I want to be filled so I can fight my battles without repenting of my sin?

In Acts 8:9–25 we see an example of someone named Simon who was asking to be filled for all the wrong reasons. "When Simon saw that the Spirit was given when the apostles laid their hands on people, he offered them money to buy this power. 'Let me have this power, too,' he exclaimed, 'so that when I lay my hands on people, they will receive the Holy Spirit!'" (vv. 18–19 NLT). In response, Peter strongly rebuked him and told him to repent for treating God's Spirit like a commodity that could be bought for personal benefit and fame.

Simon's story shows us that the Spirit's power can't be purchased. Repentance and faith are the only way to receive the Holy Spirit. He is a priceless gift given to everyone who puts their trust in Jesus.

If we want to live by the Spirit's filling and power, this is what we must remember:

> My old self has been crucified with Christ. It is no longer I who live, but Christ lives in me. So I live in this earthly body by trusting in the Son of God, who loved me and gave himself for me.
>
> Galatians 2:20 NLT

Our identity is in our union with Christ in His death and resurrection! We are empowered by the Spirit of Christ who lives in us and gives us godly desires and produces godly fruit. When He convicts us, we have a decision to make. Grieve Him or be guided by Him. Rebel against Him or let Him reign in us. The power we need to live a holy life happens when we allow the God who resides *in* us to reign *over* us!

God supplies us with the grace we need to stay in step with His Spirit. His grace given to us in Jesus saves, sanctifies, strengthens, and sustains us. His grace is how we walk filled and in freedom, my friend!

WORD

Read the full story of Simon the Magician in Acts 8:9–25. Write anything that God highlights for you about repenting of not having pure motives or godly desires when asking for His power to fill us afresh—or the times when we've wanted to experience His filling without wanting to follow His lead.

SPIRIT

I'm convicted to pause and pray. Will you join me?

Lord Jesus, reign in me!! Forgive me for my divided heart! Give me a new heart deeply devoted to being led by your Spirit so I will experience and exude the effect of your presence, and so my life would reflect your beauty and holiness!

DAY 38

How Does Prayer Foster Intimacy with God?

In Tim Keller's profound book *Prayer: Experiencing Awe and Intimacy with God*, he explains that prayer is "the main way we experience deep change—the reordering of our loves. Prayer is how God gives us so many of the unimaginable things he has for us."[1] Keller writes that prayer is awe, intimacy, struggle—yet the way to reality. There is nothing more important, or harder, or richer, or more life-altering. There is absolutely nothing so great as prayer.[2]

If we want to encounter the awe of God, to experience genuine intimacy with God, prayer is key!

There is a place and time for grappling with a theologically precise definition of prayer, but today we will stick with two of the simpler definitions, which are talking with God, and keeping company with God.

Also, though definitions of prayer vary, the *reason* we can pray does not. Why do we have unhindered access to God? Why does the writer of Hebrews say we should "with confidence draw near to the throne of grace, that we may receive mercy and find grace to help in time of need" (4:16)? The answer is Jesus, who made a way for us to come closer to a God abundant in mercy and grace! We pray through Jesus and in the name of Jesus, who said about himself, "I am the way, and the truth, and the life. No one comes to the Father except through me" (John 14:6).

But there's another important question we must answer. Who woos us to pray? Who creates in us—stubborn people prone to self-sufficiency—a desire to communicate *with* God? The Holy Spirit!

When you feel compelled to pray, may you recognize that your desire is produced by the Spirit. His presence in us propels us to pray. He draws us into the intimacy of the Trinity through communication.

Not only does He woo us to pray but He guides us in prayer *and* prays on our behalf. When Scripture comes to mind as you pray, that is the Holy Spirit giving you God-breathed words to pray back to your Father. When nothing comes to mind, or you feel too weary to utter words, or your heart hurts too much to hope, the "Spirit intercedes for the saints according to the will of God" (Romans 8:27). You are the saint He prays for! And He prays in harmony with God's will.

But maybe you wonder if your prayers matter. If every day was planned before one of them came to be, as King David writes in Psalm 139:16, we might be tempted to neglect prayer or make it our last resort. But I love how, in the next sentence, David declares, "How precious to me are your thoughts, O God!" (v. 17).

Are God's thoughts precious to us? A recent situation with my son Andre convicted me about this.

I'd texted Andre because his birthday was approaching and I wanted to mail his gifts to him at college so they arrived on time. The following day I received a response: "Hey mom, this is what I'd like for my birthday," and he attached a Word document. I giggled because ever since Andre joined our family from a children's home in Haiti, he has hesitated to give us a lot of gift ideas, even though we assure him we love giving our boys good gifts. (I wonder if we do this with God? He tells us to "pray about everything,"[a] but we don't want to ask for too much or seem too greedy!)

Well, I opened the document, prepared to place several orders for Andre's birthday. But what I read wasn't a list of presents; it was a list of prayer requests. Andre's document contained all the things he wanted

a. Philippians 4:6–7 reference.

Mike and me to pray for as he prepares to graduate from college and begin his next season of life. God's thoughts about and plans for his life are *that* precious to Andre! *And*, Andre's thoughts are *that* precious to God.

Is it hard for you to believe that your innermost thoughts and desires are precious to God? Friend, if it matters to you, it matters to Him. You cannot find a sentence in Scripture where God trivializes or dismisses the honest cry of a person's heart. He wants you to bring your longings to Him, and He bends down to hear you.[b] This is where closeness with Him and confidence in Him grow.

Praying is a way of saying, "I cannot handle this on my own and I am choosing to trust you." It's a way of acknowledging that we are not in control and we don't always know what's best. This means there will be times when God not only answers our prayer as we'd hoped, but He exceeds them. And this means that sometimes we will shake our fist and soak our pillow with tears for what remains unchanged. In these painful times, the most helpful thing I know to do is retrace His faithfulness. I rehearse Scripture that reminds me of His withness. I imagine His nail-scarred hands catching my tears. I surrender the outcome (at least I try to!) to a God who hasn't failed me yet. And I remember that Christ-conformity, even through suffering, is evidence of His "for us" love.

He is more than able to redeem circumstances He didn't change as we'd hoped He would. Beautifying is what He does. The enemy's plans for evil will not prevail. God's purposes will! We will be with Him and we will be like Him and every tear will be wiped away and every wrong will be made right. This is our sure hope. Until then, we get to draw near with every need, pleading for His will to be done.

One of the reasons I love the "talking *with* God" definition of prayer is because it emphasizes two-way communication. When we understand prayer this way, continual conversation with Jesus throughout the day becomes a way of life! Just as you wouldn't keep silent with a friend you spend the day with, you will learn to engage with Him as naturally as

b. Psalm 116:2 reference.

you would your closest friend. The biggest difference, of course, is that Jesus is the *one* Friend whose presence empowers you with everything you need for life. Intimacy and trust are cultivated in this back-and-forth with Him.

But there's one more kind of prayer that I'd be remiss not to mention, because, ultimately, prayer is not about extracting but investing in a relationship that will see us through the storms of life. If intimacy is not being cultivated through prayer, we have to ask ourselves if we *go* to Him only to *get* from Him, or if we go to Him to go deeper with Him. There is no guilt in wanting to "get" because He has *so* much to give. But the greatest gift is himself.

In Psalm 37:4, King David writes, "Delight yourself in the LORD, and he will give you the desires of your heart."

When I read that verse as a child, I thought, "I will delight in God, and He will give me everything I want." I didn't yet understand that *by* delighting in God, the desires of my heart would align with His desires for my life. Even better, delighting in God is how He becomes the ultimate desires of our heart! This is how He reorders our loves and dismantles our idols! Delighting in God deepens our connection with Him.

Delighting in God is how He becomes the ultimate desire of our heart, how He reorders our loves and dismantles our idols.

Praying this way could be called contemplative prayer. "Put simply, the contemplative life is the steady gaze of the soul upon the God who loves us. It is 'an intimate sharing between friends,' to use the words of Teresa of Avila," writes Richard J. Foster.[3]

Contemplative prayer is described by Richard Plass and James Cofield as "a willingness to enjoy and be present to God. It is a matter of being consciously aware of my presence in Christ and attentive to Christ's presence in me. It is saying yes to God with my whole being but without words."[4]

This means making time for prayer with the purpose of captivation with Christ. Be enthralled by His beauty and holiness and love. Look into His eyes and let down your guard; let His love wash over you. Setting our attention and affection on God fills us with peace, and hope, and even happiness of heart, and brings ever-increasing intimacy with Him.

God wants to show us His power through our prayer! When we pray, let's linger. Let's listen. And let a deeper life with God be ours through adoration and honest communication with Him!

WORD

Read 1 Thessalonians 5:16–18. To "pray without ceasing" advises continual fellowship with God. Ongoing communication. A preoccupation with His presence as you go through your day! Journal what this could look like in your daily life.

SPIRIT

Thank the Holy Spirit for praying on your behalf. Thank Him for praying in perfect alignment with God's will for your life. Now invite Him to well up in you the same prayer Jesus prayed to His Father, "Not my will but yours be done." As we take everything to God in prayer, and grow in connection, may our hearts be moved to even deeper trust of Him.

DAY 39

How Does God Speak to Me?

A friend texted me, "Can you talk?" I called her right away, but before I could say "Hey, friend," she exclaimed, "Jeannie, you won't believe this. Actually, you will! Do you remember when I told you God is speaking so clearly to me through Scripture like I've never experienced before? Well, today I got an email from an old friend I haven't spoken to in years. But yesterday, as she was reading her Bible, she felt God compel her to email me a specific passage. She didn't know why, and she confessed she might seem crazy, but she followed the Spirit's nudge and emailed me. Jeannie, what she sent is exactly what God has been saying to me in Scripture! I feel so seen and loved by Him!"

Some might call this coincidence. I say it was clear communication from God. Not only did my friend hear from God, she felt seen and loved by Him.

This friend has walked closely with God for a long while. But hearing from Him has always felt foreign to her. She'd confess there have been times she thought it *might* be Him speaking but she wouldn't have banked on it. How does one *really* know it's God?

In the Old Testament, God spoke through prophets. In the New Testament, Jesus is the ultimate and final prophet through whom God spoke.[a]

a. Hebrews 1:1–4 reference.

But what about today? How does God speak to you and me, and how do we know it's Him? Jesus begins to answer this question when He says to His disciples,

> But when he, the Spirit of truth, comes, he will guide you into all the truth. He will not speak on his own; he will speak only what he hears, and he will tell you what is yet to come. He will glorify me because it is from me that he will receive what he will make known to you.
>
> John 16:13–14 NIV

God the Father, God the Son, and God the Holy Spirit are one. They never disagree, and their voices never vary. God the Son and God the Spirit always speak and work in ways consistent with their respective eternal relations with God the Father. The Father speaks through the Son and in the Spirit, who can be trusted to always say only what He hears from God; and it will always glorify Him.

So when Jesus said the Spirit will guide us into all "the truth," He was speaking about himself. Jesus, the Word who became flesh, is "the truth." This means the Holy Spirit speaks to us about Jesus through Scripture. And we always must test what we sense from the Spirit with what Scripture says.

So what does the voice of God sound like? The Word of God! The more time we spend with Him in the Word, the more easily we will distinguish His voice.

Jesus taught on our ability to hear His voice.

> My sheep hear my voice, and I know them, and they follow Me.
>
> John 10:27

You are *known*—fully and completely—by Jesus. God knows His kids intimately and He is fiercely protective of them. (Any parent can relate to this!) He speaks to us personally to lead us in a full, deep life. We can recognize His voice because we've learned it through Scripture and we follow Him because we know He's trustworthy!

The Spirit also speaks to us through prayer, a prophetic word,* a Spirit-filled friend, a song lyric, a dream. At times, thoughts or words can come to mind that we sense are the Spirit speaking. His is a voice that is *in* us but is not *from* us. The Spirit can even speak through a stranger. God can be infinitely creative in how He communicates. And when we wonder if it's Him, we can hold it up to His Word.

God designed you, so He knows how to communicate with you. Yes, you must learn His voice, but this simply means building a relationship with Him, getting to know His ways, His character, His purposes, His love. The entirety of Christian life is about getting to know Him more and more, and this happens in two-way communication! Read His Word and respond. Listen for His voice and lean in when He speaks. Stay alert to His activity and join in His purposes.

Maybe it seems too bold to expect the God who spoke the world into existence to speak directly into your life. But this kind of familiarity with God's voice *is* available to each of us! The closer you get, the clearer His voice becomes. He wants to guide you in all He has prepared for your beautiful life, to bring Him glory.

The Psalmist assures us,

> The LORD directs the steps of the godly. He delights in every detail of their lives.
>
> Psalm 37:23 NLT

The godly are those seeking God. If you are seeking Him, He will direct you. We can ask, "What's next, Father?" and have confidence He will lead us on the path of life, righteousness, and peace for His name's sake.

Still, you might be asking, "But how do we *really* know it's God?"

I'll start with what might feel like bad news. We won't always know. Sometimes I've had to say, "Lord, I don't hear you or I don't know if what I'm hearing is from you. Even though it aligns with Scripture I wonder if it's your will in this situation. So I'm going to proceed and I'm asking you to protect me or halt these plans if this isn't your best for us."

Now here's the good news: We can take comfort in knowing there isn't anything God can't correct or protect or redeem! I've experienced this when I've been guilty of convincing myself it's Him speaking when it's not, especially when I've wanted the answer to be "yes" or "proceed" when I knew in my spirit it was "no" or "wait."

Also, there will be times we hear Him incorrectly. For example, when my husband and I are making a decision, we both pray about it. But sometimes we don't come to the same conclusion. One of us will have peace and one won't. But we know God can't contradict himself and He wouldn't tell us different things, so we need to assess our hearts. Are our own agendas or motives getting in the way?

And how do we know if what we're hearing is just our conscience or if it's God's Spirit? Start here: Our conscience gives us a pass on something the Spirit would not. It only carries us so far, especially one governed by an unrenewed heart![b] It can't be trusted because it is corrupted with sin and informed by our circumstances.[c]

Can the Holy Spirit use our consciences to convict us? Absolutely. Can He conform our consciences to God's? He can and does! "We have the mind of Christ," Paul assures us in 1 Corinthians 2:16. A person indwelt with the Spirit has the mind of Christ and can *learn* to hear the Spirit's voice and know His nudge.

The Holy Spirit also speaks by helping us recall what we have read in Scripture. This is why we need to be steeped in the Word, so we will never be powerless in fighting sin or lacking an inspired word to share, and always able to meditate on the truth that brings life and peace.[d]

A few simple practices to discern if what you're hearing is from God:

Ask yourself, *Does it grow me in His likeness and does it bring God glory?*

Take it to your people, those who walk in Word + Spirit, for discernment.

Ask yourself, *Does it align with the Word of God and character of God?*

b. Titus 1:15 reference.
c. Hebrews 10:22 reference.
d. John 14:25–27 reference.

Consider if there have been multiple confirmations that it's Him speaking.

And finally, practice!

Start with the small stuff. Ask Him every question that comes to mind. Don't wait for the big stuff. Just talk to Him. "Jesus, what do you think about this?" "Jesus, I really need your help with this." "Jesus, I trust you're in control of this." Keep the conversation going. And be expectant.

Then, *really* pay attention. Too often, I believe, He speaks but we weren't paying attention. The supernatural broke into the natural, and we missed it! Practice saying out loud, "I see you, God! I hear you! I love you, God!" When you believe you've encountered Him, smile and thank Him!

Being sensitive to the Spirit's speaking is essential to God's plan unfolding in our lives! It's a mind-blowing privilege of being His child.

WORD

* Prophecy, which I mentioned today, is not a product of the prophet. Prophecy is a product of God through the Holy Spirit; 2 Peter 1:21 teaches, "For no prophecy was ever produced by the will of man, but men spoke from God as they were carried along by the Holy Spirit." The Greek word translated "carried" is *phero*. They were moved along by the Holy Spirit who spoke from God. This is a gift the Holy Spirit gives believers today. It can be defined simply as truth-telling. As with any gift from the Spirit, it must be held up to Scripture. The Spirit never gives a wrong word, but people sometimes do.

SPIRIT

Consider the practical ways I offered for discerning if God is speaking and journal your thoughts. Invite the Holy Spirit to bring you undeniable encounters with your living God!

DAY 40

What Is God's Invitation to Me?

God's desire is for us to enjoy His manifest presence and be led in His mighty power. But if this is true, and we know it is, one question we might still be wrestling with is, "What about those times when God's presence feels distant and His voice seems silent?"

I have certainly known these periods in my own life. Times when I have prayed so hard to feel His palpable presence, or receive His guidance in a decision, or hear His voice speak into a situation—and all I've felt was nothing. All I've heard was crickets.

I haven't always felt Him, seen Him, or heard Him. And I've wondered if something I'd done, or was doing, was preventing me from experiencing His presence, or whether that's just how it is sometimes. Are we bold enough to say that remaining silent doesn't seem like something a good and generous God would do? Maybe it even feels cruel and inconsistent with His character.

We already know that disobedience to God can lead to our feeling distant from God. Intentional, insistent sin impedes intimacy. But what about those times when we feel we are in step with the Spirit and are repenting of our rebellion, when we are seeking Him earnestly, but God still feels distant or silent? What do we do then?

First, we need to know there *will* be times of silence. We shouldn't be surprised, and we can't believe the enemy's lies, when God's presence is felt very little or not at all. When the silence feels deafening, the enemy will tempt you to wonder if the Spirit has left the building—or better said, the temple—entirely. (You being the temple, of course.)

It's vital to understand that silence is not always an indication of being out of step with the Spirit, that it's never an indication that you've been abandoned, and that it's certainly not a new thing.

So many of the psalms were written in distress that God was hiding or had removed His hand. Just one example is in Psalm 22:1–2, where King David cries out,

> My God, my God, why have you forsaken me?
> Why are you so far from saving me, from the words of my groaning?
> O my God, I cry by day, but you do not answer,
> and by night, but I find no rest.

David feels forgotten by God. He's crying out in desperation for something, anything, to assure Him God is near. But then his pleading turns to praise in verses 3–4.

> Yet you are holy,
> enthroned on the praises of Israel.
> In you our fathers trusted;
> they trusted, and you delivered them.

It wasn't answers or a felt sense of God's presence that changed David's posture and lament. Instead, he declared God's character and rehearsed His faithfulness in the past. David not only demonstrates how we can be brutally honest with God, but he also shows us how remembering *who* God is helps us trust His withness even when we don't sense it.

The prophet Isaiah is another example of someone who expressed angst over a longing for God's presence that felt absent when he wrote, "You have hidden your face from us" (Isaiah 64:7). We know God is Spirit and not limited by an actual body, so when Scripture applies human characteristics to God, the author is expressing a spiritual rather than a physical reality. When Isaiah says God has hidden His face, he is saying he feels forsaken by God. Yet earlier, in chapter 55, Isaiah describes the invitation to come to God and be satisfied by Him alone, showing us how forgetful we are and how faithful He is.

Let's go through portions of Isaiah 55 together to remember what we've been offered in Christ!

> Come, everyone who thirsts,
> come to the waters;
> and he who has no money,
> come, buy and eat!
> Come, buy wine and milk
> without money and without price.
>
> v. 1

Do you see the grace in these verses? The invitation to drink is to every single one of us who is thirsty for God. It isn't predicated on what we have or what we lack, or on what we've done or wish we hadn't done. Thirst is all we need. The bounty is free. "Wine and milk" are symbols of abundance, enjoyment, and nourishment! We have complete access to God and these gifts not because we are good but because He is gracious and generous.

> Incline your ear, and come to me;
> hear, that your soul may live;
> and I will make with you an everlasting covenant,
> my steadfast, sure love for David.
>
> v. 3

Do you see the invitation to relationship in these verses? Come to Him for the life your soul longs for. Lean into His loving welcome. Listen for His voice. He is speaking. Are you listening?

> Seek the LORD while he may be found;
> call upon him while he is near;

> let the wicked forsake his way,
> and the unrighteous man his thoughts;
> let him return to the LORD, that he may have compassion
> on him,
> and to our God, for he will abundantly pardon.
>
> vv. 6–7

Do you see the invitation to repentance and holiness in these verses? Turn from your sin and the ways of your old life. Return to Jesus. Again and again. Seek Him. He wants to be found by you. Call upon Him. He will shower you with compassion. This abundant forgiveness will be the catalyst for your forsaking your old ways and embracing His.

> For my thoughts are not your thoughts,
> neither are your ways my ways, declares the Lord.
> For as the heavens are higher than the earth,
> so are my ways higher than your ways
> and my thoughts than your thoughts.
>
> vv. 8–9

Do you see the invitation to trust Him in these verses? We serve a God who is omnipotent (all-powerful), omniscient (all-knowing) and omnipresent (present everywhere all the time). The three *omni* attributes of God affirm that even when He seems silent or His presence isn't sensed, He is here, nothing is outside His authority, and nothing takes Him by surprise.

Ultimately, the Christian life is not anchored in feeling, but in faith. In seasons of silence, or times when we don't sense His withness, He can multiply our faith as we follow Him into the unknown. Our faith is stretched when we take Him at His Word. Our faith is strengthened when He carries us through suffering. We can walk by faith, knowing His promises are eternal and worthy of our complete trust. "And without faith it is impossible to please him, for whoever would draw near to God must believe that he exists and that he rewards those who seek him" (Hebrews 11:6).

Draw near to God! He rewards those who seek Him with himself! With His personal presence!

One of the things I've found to be true in my own life is that when I don't sense His presence, I long for it to return. Said differently, I miss Him. A lot. And I can't help but wonder if I'd take His withness for granted if there weren't days when it felt distant. Would I long for it if I never felt less of it? Would I thirst for it if I always felt satisfied by it? I don't suggest this is why God sometimes feels silent or distant, but I *can* say that it has always reminded me of how precious His presence is to me.

Our triune God desires for us to cultivate a deep sensitivity to His withness. To have a keen attentiveness to His real, relational, recognizable presence so that we might know Him more fully, follow Him more faithfully, and bear fruit more abundantly.

This is our invitation! To deeply "know him and the power of his resurrection." To enter into the vibrancy of the Trinity and be transformed into the likeness of Jesus by the power of His Spirit! To the glory of the Father.

In this intimacy, we get glimpses of how unimaginably glorious it will be when we finally dwell with Him in eternity, in which, as written by C. S. Lewis, "every chapter is better than the one before."[1]

WORD

Open your Bible and read Psalm 105:1–4, then write verse 4 below.

SPIRIT

Ask the Holy Spirit to fill you with the fullness of God, to make His beautiful presence so incredibly precious and real to you each day. With the empowering of the Spirit, keep your eyes fixed on Him and your heart tender to Him. Thank Him for leading you into the intimacy of the Trinity and a deeper, more vibrant life with God.

PERSONAL CLOSING NOTE

It's been an honor to journey with you into deeper intimacy with God.

As I write this closing note to you, I am struck by something God is newly impressing on me. It's as though He is leading me to share something that seems so simple but feels so profound to my own heart in this moment: Enjoy Him! I implore us to enjoy Him. When we enjoy Him, we glorify Him. So pursue Him to enjoy Him. I want our lives to be marked by the pleasure of His presence!

I pray that our days together have spurred you on in the practice of repentance and the pursuit of holiness, by the power of His Spirit.

I pray that our days together have awakened you to His indwelling *and* manifest presence!

I pray that the Holy Spirit has made King Jesus increasingly beautiful to you and I pray you have come to prize His presence above all else, just as the apostle Paul did when he penned our key verse.

Let us close by reciting our key passage one more time together, inviting the Holy Spirit to make it the wholehearted cry of our hearts!

> Indeed, I count everything as loss because of the surpassing worth of knowing Christ Jesus my Lord. For his sake I have suffered the loss of all things and count them as rubbish, in order that I may gain Christ and be found in him, not having a righteousness of my own that comes from the law, but that which comes through faith in Christ, the righteousness from God that depends on faith—that I may know him and

the power of his resurrection, and may share his sufferings, becoming like him in his death, that by any means possible I may attain the resurrection from the dead.

Philippians 3:8–11

There is none like Him!

Jeannie

ACKNOWLEDGMENTS

To my literary agent, Andrew Wolgemuth: I am immensely grateful for your commitment to excellence and the integrity with which you work. I don't take for granted how good it is to have an agent whose guidance I deeply trust. It's an absolute honor—and joy—to partner with you in bringing each new book to life. Thank you.

To my editor, Jennifer Dukes Lee: What a gift it is to have you—someone whose writing I deeply admire—working with me on this message. I read your books, and was changed by them, long before you became my editor and friend! I am so grateful for your depth of wisdom, gift of storytelling, love for Jesus, and sensitivity to the Spirit, along with your brilliant editorial skills. I love working with you!

Thank you to the entire Bethany House team for partnering with me on another project. It's been a truly enjoyable experience. And a special thank-you to Sharon Hodge for her keen editorial work. Your sincere thoughtfulness (and your patience with all of my edits!) made this book everything I hoped it would be! And to Deidre Close, who has shown such genuine care for and commitment to getting this message out, thank you!! I love knowing this book is in such great hands with you and your team!

Thank you to my wonderful Trinity Church family and specifically my pastor, Ben Valentine, whose gospel-centered teaching has profoundly influenced much of what I've written in these pages.

To my parents, Bonnie and George Callahan: Your profound influence on my faith is most evident in this book. You modeled for me not only a deep love for Jesus, but a deep love for the Word. I know that it's the Holy Spirit who brings Scripture to memory as I write, but it was you who raised me in the Word and it was you who led me in memorizing Scripture since my childhood. It's you who gave me a storehouse of Scripture that gives the Spirit material to work with. As the Holy Spirit has brought memorized Scripture to mind as I've written on varying topics in this book, I've been whispering my gratitude to Jesus for the gift of being raised by you. Because of you, there has never been a day that I didn't know I was loved by Jesus. And because of you, His Word is hidden in my heart. There is truly no greater gift you could have given me, and I love you so much.

To my family, my party of seven: I love us so much! To my husband, Mike, who so selflessly supports me in all the ways: When I need to hunker down in the home office for hours a day, weeks on end, and nobody gets fed and I look like the walking dead, just to meet a deadline, you are consistently there to cheer me on and remind me it's worth it. I could not do this (no, truly, I couldn't!) without your encouragement and love. It feels like your name should be on the spine with mine. Thank you for helping me follow the call of Jesus on my life. I love you with all of me. And to my extraordinary boys—Finn, Owen, Brennan, Cal, and Andre: Good grief, I love being your mama! Thank you for popping your head into my office when my face is in my Bible and my fingers are glued to the keyboard to tell me you're proud of me. Thank you for praying for me as I write. Thank you for letting me tell stories about our family that will help others find and follow Jesus. Being your mama is my greatest joy and highest honor. I love you beyond.

And finally, Jesus. My Savior. My Lord. The lover of my soul. And the coolest guy I know. This book is about you and for you. Thank you for inviting me to write books that make much of you. The longer I follow you, the more I love you. May you be so glorified in these pages! You are worthy, Jesus.

ENDNOTES

Day 1: Why Can I Experience Intimacy with God?

1. A.W. Tozer, *The Knowledge of the Holy: The Attributes of God: Their Meaning in the Christian Life* (New York: HarperCollins, 1961), 1.

Day 4: What Does Pentecost Mean for Me?

1. Jada Edwards presented this idea during her talk "Jesus: The Answer to Every Thirst" at IF: Gathering, February 24, 2024, in Fort Worth, Texas.

Day 5: Does God Manifest Himself in Me?

1. Civilla D. Martin, "His Eye Is on the Sparrow," 1905, in *Family Worship Hymnal* (Arlington Heights, IL: Christian Liberty Press, 2005), 123.

2. "manifest," *Oxford Dictionary of Difficult Words*, Archie Hobson, ed. (New York: Oxford University Press), 265.

Day 7: How Does the Spirit Foster Intimacy with God?

1. Phylicia Masonheimer, "May His Abundance Never Scare You," *Every Woman a Theologian*, n.d., https://phyliciamasonheimer.com/may-his-abundance-never-scare-you/.

Day 9: What Determines Depth of Intimacy with God?

1. Joel Muddamalle, @muddamalle, Instagram, October 31, 2022, https://www.instagram.com/p/CkYWeTopOSo/?img_index=1.

Day 10: How Do I Know I Am Growing in Intimacy with God?

1. John Piper, "How Do You Define Joy?," *Desiring God*, July 25, 2015, https://www.desiringgod.org/articles/how-do-you-define-joy.

Day 11: What Does Intimacy with God Produce in Us?

1. ESV Gospel Transformation Bible, Commentary on John 4 (Wheaton, IL: Crossway, 2011), 1414.

Day 13: Does God Really Want to Be Found by Me?

1. Jodie Berndt, *Praying the Scriptures for Your Marriage: Trusting God with Your Most Important Relationship* (Grand Rapids, MI: Zondervan, 2023), 110.

Day 14: What Is Repentance?

1. Timothy Keller, *Forgive: Why Should I and How Can I?* (New York: Viking, 2022), 149.
2. Jennie Allen presented this definition of confession on the *WHOA That's Good Podcast* with Sadie Robertson Huff, February 21, 2024, https://www.youtube.com/watch?v=yHbZUuSq2P0.

Day 15: Who Leads Us to Repentance?

1. "Disputation on the Power and Efficacy of Indulgences," *Blue Letter Bible*, https://www.blueletterbible.org/Comm/luther_martin/theses/95theses.cfm.
2. "3076. Lupeó," Thayer's Greek Lexicon STRONGS NT 3076: λυπέω, *Bible Hub*, https://biblehub.com/greek/3076.htm.

Day 16: What Leads Us to Repentance?

1. "The Connection Between Your Earthly Parents and Your Heavenly Father," Relationship IQ Blog, Boone Center for the Family, Pepperdine University, June 16, 2020, https://boonecenter.pepperdine.edu/relationship-iq/blog/posts/connection_between_your_earthly_parents_and_your_heavenly_father.htm.

Day 17: What Are the Benefits of Repentance?

1. "4383. Prosópon," Strong's Concordance, *Bible Hub*, https://biblehub.com/greek/4383.htm.

Day 19: How Do I Repent?

1. ESV Gospel Transformation Bible, Commentary on Psalm 51 (Wheaton, IL: Crossway, 2011), 700.
2. ESV Gospel Transformation Bible, 700.
3. Alicia Britt Chole, @aliciabrittchole, Instagram, January 19, 2024. https://www.instagram.com/p/C2TOKhAq2NE/.
4. The prayer was adapted from this version, found at *The (Online) Book of Common Prayer*, "A Penitential Order: Rite One," https://www.bcponline.org.

Day 20: How Do I Run the Race Well?

1. Rick Renner, *Sparkling Gems from the Greek Vol. 1: 365 Greek Word Studies for Every Day of the Year to Sharpen Your Understanding of God's Word* (Tulsa, OK: Teach All Nations, 2012), 114.

2. Jon Bloom, "Lay Aside Every Weight," *Desiring God*, April 5, 2013, https://www.desiringgod.org/articles/lay-aside-every-weight.

3. D. Martyn Lloyd-Jones, *Spiritual Depression: Its Causes and Its Cure* (Grand Rapids, MI: Eerdmans Publishing Company, 1965), 88.

4. ESV Gospel Transformation Bible, Commentary on Philippians 3 (Wheaton, IL: Crossway, 2011), 1601.

Day 22: What Is the Significance of Word + Spirit?

1. RT Kendall, "When Word and Spirit Come Together, Revival Will Follow," *Premier Christianity*, August 18, 2019, https://www.premierchristianity.com/features/rt-kendall-when-word-and-spirit-come-together-revival-will-follow/3845.article.

Day 23: How Does the Word Impact Intimacy with God?

1. "The Glorifying Ministry of the Holy Spirit," Renner.org, June 20, 2023, https://renner.org/article/the-glorifying-ministry-of-the-holy-spirit/.

2. "The Nicene Creed," The Gospel Coalition, https://www.thegospelcoalition.org/publication-online/nicene-creed/.

Day 24: How Does the Word Impact Obedience to God?

1. ESV Gospel Transformation Bible, Commentary on Thessalonians 4 (Wheaton, IL: Crossway, 2011), 1618.

2. ESV Gospel Transformation Bible, Commentary on Thessalonians 5 (Wheaton, IL: Crossway, 2011), 1620.

Day 25: What's the Difference Between the Law and the Gospel?

1. Wyatt Graham, "Martin Luther: Getting the Law and Gospel Right," The Gospel Coalition, March 15, 2021, https://ca.thegospelcoalition.org/columns/detrinitate/martin-luther-getting-the-law-and-gospel-right/.

2. Graham, "Martin Luther."

3. Graham, "Martin Luther."

4. Michael Horton, "Law and Gospel," Ligonier, October 1, 2006, https://www.ligonier.org/learn/articles/law-and-gospel.

Day 28: What Is Freedom in Christ?

1. "3306. menó," Thayer's Greek Lexicon, *Bible Hub*, https://biblehub.com/greek/3306.htm.

Day 30: What Is Holiness?

1. Steven Lawson, "What Is the Holiness of God?," Ligonier, February 26, 2021, https://www.ligonier.org/learn/articles/holy-one-god.

2. Lawson, "What Is the Holiness of God?"

Day 31: What Is the Holy Spirit's Role in Holy Living?

1. ESV Gospel Transformation Bible, Commentary on Thessalonians 4 (Wheaton, IL: Crossway, 2011), 1618.

2. Macrina Wiederkehr, *Seasons of Your Heart: Prayers & Reflections* (Morristown, NJ: Silver Burdett & Ginn, 1979), 60.

Day 32: How Do I Grow in Holiness?

1. ESV Gospel Transformation Bible, Commentary on 2 Corinthians 3 (Wheaton, IL: Crossway, 2011), 1558.

Day 33: Why Do I Drift?

1. Robert Robinson, "Come, Though Fount of Every Blessing," 1758, public domain, Hymnary.org, https://hymnary.org/text/come_thou_fount_of_every_blessing.

Day 34: Why Does Jesus Tell Me to Deny Myself?

1. Jon Bloom, "The Secret to Breaking Free from Habitual Sin," *Desiring God*, June 29, 2019, https://www.desiringgod.org/articles/the-secret-to-breaking-free-from-habitual-sin.

Day 35: Why Does God Command My Worship?

1. C. S. Lewis, *Reflections on the Psalms* (New York: Harcourt, Brace & Co., 1958), 108. Extracts used with permission.

2. Lewis, *Reflections on the Psalms*, 111. Extracts used with permission.

3. Sam Storms, "How C. S. Lewis Changed the Way I Worship," *Enjoying God*, October 7, 2013, https://www.samstorms.org/enjoying-god-blog/post/how-c--s--lewis-changed-the-way-i-worship.

4. Lewis, *Reflections on the Psalms*, 112. Extracts used with permission.

Day 36: How Does the Holy Spirit Fill Me?

1. "Be filled (4137) (pleroo)," Ephesians 5:17–18 Commentary, Precept Austin, https://www.preceptaustin.org/ephesians_517-18#5:18.

Day 37: What If I Don't Feel His Filling?

1. Tim Keller, *Prayer: Experiencing Awe and Intimacy with God* (New York: Penguin, 2016), 62.

Day 38: How Does Prayer Foster Intimacy with God?

1. Tim Keller, *Prayer: Experiencing Awe and Intimacy with God* (New York: Penguin, 2016), 18.
2. Keller, *Prayer*, 32.
3. Richard J. Foster, *Streams of Living Water: Essential Practices from the Six Great Traditions of Christian Faith* (New York: HarperSanFrancisco, 1998), 49.
4. Richard Plass and James Cofield, *The Relational Soul: Moving from False Self to Deep Connection* (Madison, WI: IVP Books, 2014), 143.

Day 40: What Is God's Invitation to Me?

1. C. S. Lewis, *The Last Battle* (New York: HarperCollins, Reprint edition, 2002), 228. Extracts used with permission.

JEANNIE CUNNION is a bestselling author and Bible teacher whose books and Bible studies include *Mom Set Free*, *Don't Miss Out*, and *Never Alone*. She has been featured on outlets such as the *TODAY* show, *Fox News*, CBN, *Proverbs 31 Ministries*, *Christianity Today*, and *Focus on the Family*. Jeannie has a master's degree in social work and is the cofounder of The 509 Foundation, which seeks to create opportunities for children in Haiti to pursue lives of impact. Jeannie lives in Greenwich, Connecticut, with her husband, Mike, and their five boys. Connect with her at JeannieCunnion.com.